Developing Writing for Different Purposes:

Teaching about Genre in the Early Years

Developing Writing for Different Purposes:

Teaching about Genre in the Early Years

Jeni Riley and David Reedy

P·C·P
Paul Chapman
Publishing Ltd

Paul Chapman Publishing Ltd
A SAGE Publications Company
6 Bonhill Street
London EC2A 4PU

SAGE Publications Inc
2455 Teller Road
Thousand Oaks, California 91320

SAGE Publications India Pvt Ltd
32, M-Block Market
Greater Kailash - I
New Delhi 110 048

British Library Cataloguing in Publication data
A catalogue record for this book is available from the British Library

ISBN 0 7619 6463 0
ISBN 0 7619 6464 9 (pbk)

Library of Congress catalog card number available

Typeset by Anneset, Weston-super-Mare, Somerset
Printed and bound by Athenaeum Press, Gateshead

For Benjamin, William, Tess, Sean and Alice

Contents

Foreword
by Professor Gunther Kress

I have a longstanding interest in the notion of genre; in fact I can date it quite precisely, to a day in October 1979 when I was finishing a book on how children came to writing. I was then living and working in Adelaide. Over the next twelve years I worked together with many people in Australia in developing an understanding of genre, as a means of making the knowledge involved in successful writing as explicit as it could be made. It seemed to the people in the Australian 'Genre-School' that in a multicultural society, considerations of equity simply demanded that such knowledge should be as explicitly there as it could possibly be, in a curriculum of writing, for every member of the classroom, no matter what their cultural background. Only in that way could 'access' be ensured, access to the whole curriculum, but access also to the cultural, social, political, and economic goods of the society in which they lived. It is a great pleasure therefore to see these ideas beginning to have their effect in the UK. Of course they have needed translation – on the one hand for practitioners in the classroom (a task also undertaken in Australia) and for the similar and different social conditions of this country. That translation requires special skill, special knowledge, and special experience, which the authors of this volume clearly do have. The tasks of bringing this knowledge to teachers are worthwhile and necessary: and it is performed excellently and with insight in this book. I hope that it has its desired effects, and will add its weight and its voice to a gathering body of useful knowledge around writing and reading, to the benefit of the young people in our schools.

Gunther Kress
Professor in Education
with special reference to the teaching of English
June 1999

Acknowledgements

Jeni Riley and David Reedy would like to thank those children who have helped their thoughts about writing to develop through the production of this book. We are especially grateful to the five whom we know best of all, Benjamin, William, Tess, Sean and Alice, for the contribution they have made to our understanding of the literacy process.

Our sincere gratitude goes also to the pupils of Dorothy Barley Infant School and Monteagle Primary School in the London Borough of Barking and Dagenham. Their whole-hearted generosity in sharing their work makes this book what it is.

Introduction

Children should be taught written language, not just the writing of letters. (Vygotsky,1978:119)

Both our lives are deeply concerned with the teaching of literacy. Jeni Riley has spent a great deal of her career teaching children to read and write, thinking about, researching into and lecturing on the teaching of literacy. David Reedy, initially as a class teacher, and now as an advisory teacher, continues to explore the processes involved in teaching children to read and write. He works alongside teachers in order to support them in their teaching and their pupils as they learn to become literate.

This is a book that we believed it was important for us to write. It addresses the multifaceted nature of the writing process and its close relationship with reading, particularly in the early years of schooling. We discuss how the sometimes competing demands that writing makes on the young child can be overwhelming. Conversely, we know that young children are extraordinarily capable and that being able to operate within written language can both increase their intellectual capacity and provide a mode of transmission of thoughts to others.

Enabling pupils to become fluent in their use of written language therefore necessitates an approach to teaching that concentrates on the interdependent but distinct aspects of writing, of which being able to represent the sounds of speech in print is one. However, our main concern in this volume is how best to enable children to structure their writing so that it both takes into consideration the absent reader and adheres to the cultural conventions of discourse and form for different cultural purposes. Effective teaching and learning follow deep understanding of what the child knows and can do. What we offer is a discussion of the approaches that teachers can use to assess children's developing ability to write both to express themselves clearly and with a growing awareness of the appropriate form for specific genre.

The principles that underpin this book on the teaching of writing in the early years of school are that:

- the acquisition of literacy is life-enhancing
- writing is the complementary process to reading
- the development of each language mode is interrelated and supportive of the other
- as children learn to read and write their powers of thinking are developed
- for children and adults writing is difficult.

The acquisition of literacy is life-enhancing

Literacy offers opportunities for personal growth, for an improved quality of life, for an enhanced self-image and the ability to function in the world. Being literate gives individuals access to knowledge and to an increasingly information-rich world, and this in turn provides choices which can lead to self-fulfilment.

Writing is the complementary process to reading

Literacy is a complex, multifaceted process, with reading being the way of decoding and writing the way of encoding the sounds of speech into print. Hence, children are greatly supported by their reading as they learn to write. The reverse is also true – experience of reading texts of different types enables the production of various texts for many purposes. We believe that teachers can capitalize to great effect on this complementarity of reading and writing. As they work out how to transfer the sounds of speech into written language, young children gain access to the alphabetic code aspect of writing. This understanding is fundamental to fluent reading and writing.

The development of each language mode is interrelated and supportive of the other

Not only do the two modes of written language interact with each other to great mutual benefit, the development of oracy also supports the development of literacy. Whilst there are substantial differences between the modes of written and spoken language, there are parallels in the way that individuals learn to speak and learn to read and write – not least the notion of the context for learning needing to be rooted in meaningful activities. Children learn to talk when they have a genuine purpose for communicating. The same principle is true with literacy, particularly with writing, which, we argue, requires very high levels of motivation.

As children learn to read and write their powers of thinking are developed

We believe along with Donaldson and Reid that the acquisition of literacy is 'the main road, for the child's mind, out of the situation-bound, embedded thinking and language of the pre-literate years into a new kind of mental power and freedom' (1985:240). When children learn to read they have personal access to a wider, richer vocabulary as they experience literary language. They meet new ideas and information, and importantly, they have experience of the formal and often high-status modes of discourse.

As children learn to write they learn to use language in new and different ways compared with the way they speak. They become more precise, the language becomes more systematic and ordered. Donaldson argues that by providing examples and ways of using language in specific forms to fulfil their own purposes, we enable children to use language that not only is required for advanced thinking but is thought-enhancing.

A step beyond this consideration, Bereiter and Scardamalia (1993) propose that there are two types of writing: one is knowledge-telling and the other is knowledge-transforming. We focus in this book on the ways that teachers can enable children to write in a way that transforms their own knowledge. We argue that this can be achieved if teachers provide authentic, challenging and stimulating purposes for writing, if they explore through discussion the different features of text forms, and if they model writing with the children.

The knowledge-transforming model of writing

Bereiter and Scardamalia (1993) propose that knowledge-transforming writing is a model of writing which keeps growing in complexity to match the expanding competence of the writer. As competence increases, the difficulties encountered whilst composing are replaced with new ones, and at a higher level of functioning. Bereiter and Scardamalia suggest that writing at this level goes beyond the individual's normal linguistic achievement, to enable development of her own thinking through the writing process; she is able to re-process knowledge through her own cognitive activity:

> This means going beyond the ordinary ability to put one's thoughts and knowledge into writing. It means ... being able to shape a piece of writing to achieve intended effects and to re-organise one's knowledge in the process. (1993:157)

This view of writing also looks at the way that language is taught which builds on what the child implicitly knows. As Richmond says:

> The most important job for the adults who care for the child is to help the child's implicit knowledge develop. For teachers this means providing a classroom environment which supports and affirms the child's achievements, while continually proposing activities calling forth greater powers of articulation and understanding. (1990:28)

Writing is difficult

Both children and adults find the process of writing intellectually and physically demanding. We suggest that this needs to be brought to the forefront of teachers' minds as they work with their young pupils. Their teaching needs to take into account the findings of empirical research that shed light on what is involved in the writing process; and also the extent to which children are stimulated, entranced and motivated into making the effort to express themselves in written language. It is worth the effort. 'There is something in the actual act of composing on paper that oils the juices of your cognitive processes, so that as you write, ideas take on meaning and shape' (Curruthers, 1991 cited in Smith and Elley, 1998:85).

Jeni Riley and David Reedy
June 1999

1

The Mysterious Process of Writing

The linear scribble that fills the lines of a writing pad has, for the child, all the mystery of an unfamiliar code. It stands for a myriad of possible things but does not convey a particular message. The child seems to say, 'I hope I've said something important. You must be able to understand what I've said. What did I write?'

(Clay, 1975:48)

Introduction

This quotation of Marie Clay indicates both the child's developing understanding and her anxiety about her early attempts to write, and Clay signifies the mysteriousness of the activity, as it appears to be, for very young children. One day, whilst his mother and father were busy, a conversation between an adult and a four-year-old boy, discussing how an entire morning was to be spent, went like this:

JLR: I know, let's write to Roy and tell him how sorry you are that he wasn't able to come with me and see you!
Benjamin: But, I *can't* write!

Benjamin, by this stage of his educational career, had been attending a reception class for a term. His teacher, who is admirable in many respects, writes underneath his paintings and drawings, precisely what Ben dictates. He then copies. Watching as he had on many occasions, Ben realised that he had not, as yet, mastered the code aspect of writing. He could copy the words and read them back, half recalled from memory, but encoding his own thoughts into written language currently remained a mystery to him. Although this child understood clearly what writing is and some of what it entails, he was under the impression that the alphabetic code was all that writing was about,

1

as a result of the particular approach to writing in his school. Sadly, he had never been encouraged to mark-make in order to communicate.

What do you need to know in order to be able to write?

Initially, understanding about the nature and purpose of writing develop through understandings about reading. Vygotsky (1962:98–9) clarifies the two *major* hurdles faced by a child when she writes; one is a conceptual problem and is the need to 'replace words by images of words', and the other is a practical, but abstract, problem of the need to address a person who is absent.

Is that *all* there is to know about the writing process? Sadly, no: it is not as straightforward (or as complex!) as that. The individual has also to be able to encode thought into the written symbols that represent the sounds of speech. So, before a child is able to operate the act of writing, she has to have come to appreciate at some level what is entailed; she has to have, at least, a partial recognition of the differences between speech and writing.

The differences between written and spoken language

There are distinct and important differences between oracy and literacy. Firstly, written language is used to:

1. *Communicate over time and space.* It must therefore be shaped in such a way that meaning is conveyed despite the lack of a shared physical context between writer and reader. With a conversation there is the support of the situation and the presence of the speaker, whose meaning can be negotiated through gesture and repetition; any confusion can be immediately clarified; for instance, 'Don't do that!' means nothing without knowledge or explanation of the situation in which it occurred.

2. *Make thoughts and emotions permanent* – when writing there is time to express these ideas and feelings precisely. With writing the opportunity exists to re-read and to reconsider, to order and to establish clarity. This results in the use of a literary language or vocabulary (e.g. 'he cried' instead of 'he said'), syntax (that is more complex and integrated), and reference conventions being used differently from speaking.

3. *Accommodate different degrees of involvement* between the writer and

reader. The impersonal, dislocated nature of text has to be considered by the writer in order to make the meaning clear to a reader.

4. *Record life events of importance* such as government policy statements, wills, passports, certificates of births, deaths and marriages. There is a notion of authority about print as exploited by the law such as with the formality of contracts. Gossip, jokes and travel directions are more easily and perhaps better communicated through speech which allows for mood and a listener-specific adaptation or interest and gesture.

Secondly, there are distinctions between the two language modes that are connected with their production:

1. There are formal conventions that we use when we write which have to be learned. These are equivalent to and related to the concepts about print that have to be appreciated before reading can occur. These conventions are the directionality of print, rules of punctuation, the distinction between upper and lower case letters, the use of paragraphs – none of which has any corresponding form in speech.

2. Speech appears as a continuous stream of sounds or phonemes – but when we write we make distinctions between words.

3. Speech is informal, repetitive and marked by pauses and 'spacers' such as 'er', 'um', 'y'know', 'like', 'innit?' and, increasingly fashionable, 'right?' delivered with an upward intonation at the end of a statement. These 'spacers' slow down production and make speech less dense and more easily understood. Witness the incomprehensibility of an inaugural lecture written down and read, without pauses or anecdotes for elaboration!!

4. Children have to appreciate that a word is a unit of meaning, within which there are units of sound that need to be represented by a symbol, or a series of symbols, namely letters, when writing.

The appreciation that the alphabet is a code system

The last point refers to the necessity, when learning to use written symbols, of understanding that the writing system is an artificial code. Children come to understand about writing through their, often greater, experience with reading. Literacy encompasses the twin processes of reading and writing (that is *decoding* and *encoding*) and they develop in conjunction with each other, if slightly out of step.

Learning to use written language is grafted onto the child's previous learning of speech. In Bielby's (1999) words, 'learning to read and write are parasitic on learning to speak', and the many understandings and skills acquired earlier can be utilized. Children learn to speak in order to communicate and to make meaning, and learning to read and write fulfils similar personal purposes.

The understanding regarding the nature and function of the alphabetic code is crucial to successful literacy learning. Whilst it is possible for this understanding to develop (through opportunities to engage with text and direct teaching), it can only genuinely occur after the secure establishment of the concept that print has a communicative function and that its use is governed by certain rules and conventions.

Awareness of concepts about print

Children gradually become literate over many years and through many thousands of exposures to texts and signs. The recognition that the alphabet is a symbolic system that represents the sounds of speech in a written code and that the meaning of the text can be retrieved from this code, is an exciting and life-changing one. Extensive research evidence, the majority of which will largely have to be left unacknowledged (for a detailed discussion see Riley, 1999), has shed light on the mechanisms at work in this journey of rediscovery as the child learns that spoken language is represented by written symbols in order to create text.

Before any progress on the path to literacy can be made, the child needs to appreciate, through a wealth of firsthand experience, that a written text is permanent and unchanging. This occurs mainly through the experience of reading, that is, through having stories and books read to her. Books and stories, it would seem, are still the most common vehicle through which these understandings are acquired, rather than text on a computer screen or a television. Early awareness of the unchanging nature of print is demonstrated by the furious protest when a bedtime story is brought to an abrupt end and a favourite part of the tale left out. Children of three years old and less know exactly when they have been short-changed on a re-reading of a much loved story. Following this understanding, awareness of the rules and conventions of print is the next intellectual hurdle for the child to surmount and this has to be achieved before the complexity of the code-breaking part of the literacy process can be tackled. This achievement is discussed in detail in Chapters 3 and 4.

Spoken and written language and thought

A conceptual understanding of literacy is fundamental and one that the child needs to have before reading or writing are possible. On another occasion, Benjamin indicated that he knew that literacy is linked to thinking, as his frustrated remarks showed when an adult was reading the newspaper rather than playing a (senseless!) game called 'Ker Plunk!' with him:

Benjamin: Why does it take you so long to read the paper?
JLR: Because papers are very thick on Sundays.
Benjamin: Why don't you read out loud?
JLR: Because . . .
Benjamin: I know, it's because you are just thinking it!

Thinking and literacy are fundamentally connected – Ben has worked that out at four years old. We cannot write without thinking. The act of reading and writing develops thought, yet the task of writing involves a great deal more than merely writing down one's thoughts. Inextricably related to this issue is the intriguing issue of the necessity to shape one's thinking in a writerly way, and how this is learned.

The question as to whether human beings think without words is discussed by Smith and Elley (1998) who suggest that there is no linear relationship between thought and words and that the way that the mind stores and processes thought is still somewhat unclear. Personally and anecdotally, we know that thinking can be through images and through our senses. We do not dream in words, and sometimes we have to represent ideas graphically in order to clarify to ourselves a particular problem. The simultaneity of the presentation of information on a computer screen can clarify understanding. Dancers think through a sequence of movement by actually dancing it. Spellings are tested out kinaesthetically – hand and arm muscles obey the habituated motor actions, and so produce the letters in the correct sequence. Music is composed through mentally experimenting with the notes in one's head, and so on.

The notion of thought being 'inner speech' is attributed to Vygotsky (1962:149) who suggests poetically that it is 'a dynamic, unstable thing, fluttering between word and thought'. He goes on to claim that initially thought and language are separate but at the age of around two years of age, they become joined and interrelated and thus a new cognitive behaviour is formed which serves the intellect. In this way, spoken language is, for Vygotsky, a tool which is thought-enhancing in many ways. Speech allows the infant to label objects and so to form concepts, to have social interactions with access to conversation, to share ideas and stories. In today's terms, spoken language allows children to have recourse to mind-developing experiences through film and television.

Written language has further potential to promote thought. Through the process of writing down our thoughts we order them, we clarify and expand them. Bruner (1957) suggests that thinking is developed through learning how to operate the cultural tool of written language. In extension of this idea, Donaldson (1993) is clear that the ability to read and write offers the opportunity to use a symbolic system, and that through operating within it, thought is made more systematic and ordered. It is through being able to operate in the sophisticated communication systems of an advanced society that the individual has, in turn, her thinking enhanced.

> The thinking itself draws great strength from literacy whenever it is more than a scrap of an idea, whenever there are complex possibilities to consider. It is even more obvious that the sustained, orderly communication of this kind of thinking requires considerable mastery of the written word.

> (Donaldson, 1993:50)

As children grow older, in addition, thinking is advanced by being able to read texts in which the meaning is, of necessity, 'disembedded' or free from the immediate context.

> They [children] need to learn gradually, over the school years, how to participate in the impersonal modes of thinking and of linguistic expression that are an important part of our cultural heritage. We have seen that, compared with speech, all language on the page has a quality of detachment from the personal life. But the kind of written language we are now concerned with is also more impersonal in the details of its form. It entails the use of phrases like, 'It is possible that ...' or 'The causes of this seem to lie ...' or 'One reason is ...' or 'What this means is ...'

> (Ibid. :51)

Through this exposure to written texts, the child is learning how to reason, to argue and to justify; in these ways her thinking becomes more advanced and qualitatively different.

What is involved when we write?

There are those who have attempted to explain how thought is shaped into written words – Britton (1972, 1983) is one. His categories of language functions, adopted by the influential Bullock Report (DES,

1975), *A Language for Life*, divide writing into a *poetic-expressive-trans-actional* model. Britton's categories represent a mental shaping of thought, the result of which are the three types of writing. In other words, he suggests that there are different modes of writing in order to fulfil specific language functions.

The three main categories are Transactional, Expressive and Poetic. The *Expressive* is the central one. It is 'close to the speaker', often the language used by intimates in a shared context; it provides the tentative stage through which a pupil's new thinking must pass on its way to the comparative certainty of knowledge (DES, 1975:165).

The Bullock Report considered that the primary school child needs to have both experience and mastery of each category before transferring to secondary school. One of the difficulties encountered with a task that sets out to describe exactly what the writer has to do in order to write, is that it is necessary to decide on the best sequence in which the various processes of writing should be discussed. Beard (1994) cites Hayes and Flower (1980) who liken a writer to a busy switchboard operator for whom, if difficulties occur, there is a clear need to partition the problem, without losing sight of the underlying communicative purpose. The same principle of partitioning holds true when attempting to explain the different processes that are involved in order to translate one's thoughts into a permanent text that can be read and re-read.

A useful, if rather simplistic, starting point is to make a distinction between *composition*, that is the concern with the content and how it is shaped and developed, and the *transcriptional* skills, which deal with the secretarial aspects of writing such as handwriting and spelling. Punctuation is thought to straddle both categories as it is concomitant with the syntax (grammar) and semantics (meaning) of the text.

In the case of very young children, of course (and this has been considered earlier), there is the additional requirement to know how the alphabetic code works before translation can be achieved – at any rate, *before* there can be a universal sharing of the text. Pre-school and nursery-aged children 'compose' and 'write' their thoughts but they are not accessible to others, nor often, after only a short passage of time, are they accessible to themselves! Hence Clay's quotation at the beginning of this chapter. The aspect concerned with a developing access to a written code will be addressed in Chapters 3 and 4, along with the assessment and teaching of the transcriptional skills. It is somewhat simplistic to apply a finite distinction between the secretarial skills of transcription and those of composition, as we suggested earlier, because, as any experienced writer is aware, the two components provide mutually reinforcing support for each other. However, it is the level of the writer's knowledge of discourse, i.e. which is the appropriate *type* of text dictated by the various purposes for writing, that influences the overall production of the final text. What cognitive processes are involved in the composition of text?

The processes involved in the composition of text

A mystery that remains unresolved is why, for many children and some adults, writing is such a painful, laborious process and for others, it happens so easily and with such fluency. One explanation is that this is due to the cognitive mechanism of automatization, which can be described as one in which familiarity, repetition and practice of a process greatly facilitate production. However, the work of Bereiter and Scardamalia (1993) suggests that the issue is a great deal more complex than that. On this, by way of introduction to the topic of composition, they say:

> Writing, by which we mean the composing of texts intended to be read by people not present, is a promising domain within which to study the relationship between easy and difficult cognitive functions. On the one hand, writing is a skill traditionally viewed as difficult to acquire, and one that is developed to immensely higher levels in some people than in others . . . On the other hand, it is based on linguistic capabilities that are shared by all normal members of the species. People with only the rudiments of literacy can, if sufficiently motivated, redirect their oral language abilities into producing a written text. (1993:155)

This seeming contradiction is explained by the Canadian researchers with the proposal of the existence of two different models of composition that individuals might employ, and which involve different cognitive processes. It is not a matter of degree. Both of the models can be done either well or badly. The two models of writing are *knowledge-telling* and *knowledge-transforming*.

As people who are struggling to write, it is highly relevant to us and our task in writing this book to attempt to clarify the process we are currently undertaking. The two models of writing described by Bereiter and Scardamalia are analogous to the distinction between casual reading and critical reading.

The knowledge-telling model
This model makes writing a relatively natural task, using existing cognitive structures to overcome difficulties, and to minimize the extent to which new challenges are introduced to the task. This type of

writing is closely related to the spontaneous process of speech, and the writer is relatively unreflective in its production. Language competence and skills, already mastered, are well utilized, supported by social experience, but in so doing the outcome is also limited by their use. In the knowledge-telling model, the writer produces text in a relatively straightforward, unmonitored way, unfettered by the constraints of the operation of discourse knowledge of text, the result of which, found in the knowledge-transforming model, is that writing is structured into different types of organization, in order to suit the appropriate register, mode or genre.

The knowledge-transforming model

This model makes writing a task which keeps growing in complexity to match the expanding competence of the reflective writer. As competence increases, the difficulties encountered are replaced with new ones, and they are at a higher level of functioning. It is called the 'psychology of the problematic' by Bereiter and Scardamalia, because it goes beyond the individual's normal linguistic achievement, to enable the writer to develop her own thinking through the writing process; she is able to re-process knowledge through her own cognitive activity. 'This means going beyond the ordinary ability to put one's thoughts and knowledge into writing. It means . . . being able to shape a piece of writing to achieve intended effects and to reorganize one's knowledge in the process' (1993:157).

The intended purpose of this book

The application of Bereiter and Scardamalia's theory seems to be at the very heart of this book. Teachers, by supporting children's developing understanding of genre, enable pupils both to recognize what is distinctive about the different genres and to know how to compose texts that are specific and appropriate to the types of various discourse. Teachers are laying the foundations of their pupils' control of knowledge-transforming writing. This type of writing eludes many, but is one of the most powerful tools to develop thought. In order to understand this theory clearly, it is necessary to look at the process of composition in more depth; we will now explore the mechanisms of composition and what other theorists consider to be involved.

A schematic model of expert writing

This explanation (proposed by Hayes and Flower (1980)), sees writing as a dynamic model and focuses on the productive interrelationship of the different stages within the components, as the writer begins with 'an idea, a turn of phrase, an emotion, an image and shuttles back and forth between ideas, images, emotions and words' (Smith and Elley, 1998:68). The text acts as a guide, as it is being written, for what will be written. Each sentence shapes its successor, in the way its predecessor has influenced its shape. There are three main components of composing; they are 'planning', 'translating' and ' reviewing' (Hayes and Flower, 1980).

Planning is the consideration of the content in a broad sense, of 'forming an internal representation of the knowledge that will be used in writing' (Flower and Hayes, 1981:372). Encompassed within this stage of writing is the research and reading which constitute the gestation part before planning a text with more academic writing. Planning can be broken down into sub-sections:

- generating ideas or the search of the memory bank for relevant ideas
- organizing ideas, which involves setting the ideas into a coherent structure
- goal setting, by which Flower and Hayes mean the on-going process whereby ideas are generated and the writing shapes to accommodate them. 'Refining one's goals is not limited to the "pre-writing stage" ... but is intimately bound up with the on-going, moment-to-moment process of composing' (1981:373).

Individual writers vary in the extent to which they pre-organize their text, and writing clearly is an evolving process for mature and novice alike. But prior thinking is essential, and is a stage often neglected by very young writers.

Translating involves the transference of ideas to paper or screen. This process requires the secretarial skills of handwriting or typing, knowledge of the conventions of print, the choice of appropriate vocabulary and sentence structures and spelling. It is at this stage that writing generates new ideas and thoughts. If too much effort is required for any or all of these skills, as is often the case with young children, there remains little mental capacity free to be expended on the content or the ideas being recorded.

Reviewing consists of two sub-processes which are evaluating and revising. Writing has to be read and re-read critically and then strategies put into place for revision. This can occur continuously, with the production of each sentence, or at the end of the piece. Translating and reviewing are integrated in the knowledge transformation; how they interact with each other depends on the writer's style of cognitive processing.

Finally, these processes are all *monitored* or overseen by a mechanism which controls the work as it is produced. The writer may move from translating, back to planning, and then to reviewing, several times before progress is made or the text is deemed complete.

This explanatory model is a helpful one for teachers to consider, entrusted as they are with the task of helping children to develop as writers. The Hayes and Flower model does not encompass a notion that the process of writing might vary for different types of writing or may differ from culture to culture, but nevertheless, it provides valuable insight regarding the 'in the head', composition part of the process of writing.

From conversation to knowledge-telling through to knowledge-transforming writing

In the view of Bereiter and Scardamalia (1993), certain challenges present themselves to children in the writing process. The move from oral to written expression has encompassed within it inherent difficulties. In the view of these researchers, the most fundamental and problematic of these difficulties is the absence of a conversational partner. Further challenges to children are:

- thinking what to say (content)
- staying on topic
- producing an intelligible whole (coherence)
- making choices appropriate to an audience not immediately present.

Earlier in this chapter we have addressed the issues concerned with the differences between spoken and written language, and the problems this presents to young writers. Bereiter and Scardamalia reiterate these with slightly different emphases, which are well worth our consideration:

- Children learn to speak naturally (and sometimes we wish we could stop them!), but learning to write requires learning a new set of conventions and rules. Young pupils have to learn to hold a pen, to know how to form the letters, to work out how to represent the sounds of speech with letters and groups of letters, to spell words accurately, to know which form of a letter, upper or lower case, is required and so on – and this is before we come to paragraphs, full stops, commas and other forms of punctuation.
- Removed from a listening partner, the child has to engage in new types of thought processes; she has to be able to take the reader's

perspective. With no feedback on whether what has been written is interesting, or has been understood, the writer has to anticipate any possible confusion. The message has to be completely comprehensible and able to stand on its own.

- Lastly, and most importantly for these researchers, the child has to be able to sustain her writing, without the prompts or the encouragement experienced when talking, through the function accomplished by a listener's comments in conversations. Writers quite literally 'dry up' through the lack of feedback in this isolated activity.

Bereiter and Scardamalia suggest that teachers have to support children learning to write through helping them to:

- produce continuous text without a turn-taking partner
- learn to search their memory for content
- learn to think ahead and to plan
- learn to revise their own writing.

Producing continuous text without a turn-taking partner

Research was undertaken that explored the ways children might be supported through their stumbling blocks with writing. First, it was hypothesized that part of the disparity of quantity between talking and writing was due to the effect of the burden imposed through the physical act of writing rather than the lack of feedback. Bereiter and Scardamalia (1982) conducted an experiment whereby they asked groups of children to respond to a certain topic in different modes:

(i)   talking about it
(ii) dictating what they wished to say to a scribe
(iii) writing unassisted on the same topic.

The results were as one might have anticipated: the group asked to speak produced most (on average 45 words), the group dictating to a scribe produced on average 35 words and the writing group wrote 20 words on average. Clearly, having someone to transcribe the ideas onto the page did, indeed, assist the process of production. As these experimental groups were older primary-aged pupils, it might be argued that with younger children, the difference might have been even more marked.

The second investigation had more surprising results. With the hypothesis that it is the lack of feedback that presents the greatest challenge to young writers, an experiment was designed with three conditions. Once again, three groups of nine- and ten-year-old children were given a topic and were asked to write an essay, each with different instructions and conditions:

(i)   one group received normal essay instructions
(ii)   the second group were asked to write 'as much as possible'
(iii) the third group were also asked to write 'as much as possible' but were supplied with contentless prompts such as 'Well done!', 'Keep going', 'Tell us more!' and 'This is really good!', etc.

The researchers found that the second group produced three times as much material as the first group, and the third group produced almost twice as much again. The extra prompting had a hugely positive effect on the children's writing performance, more so than the scribing had in the previous experiment. In fact, Bereiter and Scardamalia, writing in a later article, consider that it is the actual production of writing that has the effect of organizing and ordering thought and ideas and so facilitates production. Importantly for our focus in this book, the act of 'thinking aloud'/dictation lacked this cognitive aid.

Learning to search one's memory for content

The problems children have with recalling their passive information when writing are, self-evidently, not present when they are engaged in conversation. Teachers need to support young writers by offering strategies which will assist a memory search for relevant information.

A prior-to-writing brainstorming session is a well-tried method for overcoming this hurdle. The researchers conducted experiments with several modes of using this approach, and it appears that brainstorming strategies where children are prompted to think on the topic, in order to produce lists of keywords that can then act as a prompt to the memory, rather than writing whole sentences, proved to be the most valuable. Discussion is also useful, as is conferencing, in order to further explore the child's thought process, to aid information retrieval and to extend her developing ideas. All of these approaches are only valuable if they are an explicit way of demonstrating to writers how they need to go about the composition process for themselves – the strategies are merely exemplars of the way that mature writers prepare and organize their writing.

Learning to think ahead and to plan

Inexperienced writers, as they embark on the first sentence, frequently do not have any sense of the overall structure or goal for their writing.

This lack of a plan is a key feature of the knowledge-telling model of writing. Part of the difficulty is due to the limitations within the child and her level of cognitive maturity, and not being able to think of more than one thing at once. To generate ideas, to translate them into text and to revise the product, which means critically reading for appropriateness of language expression, structure and content, all of this is just too demanding a task for young children.

Writing frames are one attempt to facilitate pupils into being able to meet these multi-demands. On this side of the Atlantic, David Wray and colleagues have done much to make teachers aware of the possibilities of this way of supporting children's thinking whilst writing. We will discuss this in more detail later in Chapters 7 and 8. Bereiter and Scardamalia suggest lists of sentence openers that offer a structure for pupils and demonstrate a way to develop an argument, such as:

The first reason why . . .
Secondly . . .
A third factor . . .
On the other hand some people . . .
To sum up . . .

In addition, the approach advocated by Graves (1983), to support writing through conferencing, is a possible way forward, but in order for this technique to be valuable, as with all teaching, the teachers themselves have to be knowledgeable of the writing process and what cognitive demands it makes upon the child.

Learning to revise one's own writing

This crucial aspect that is required in order for pupils to develop as writers also appears to be a great stumbling block for primary-aged pupils. Numerous research projects, investigating an improvement in the revision aspect of the composition process, report on only developing the ability to proofread, at best, and that rather superficially. Redrafting does not occur in speech and requires considerable cognitive maturity for the individual to be able to 'decentre' and thus to envisage why a hypothetical reader might have difficulty with the text produced. One study by Bereiter and Scardamalia (1982) did produce results that look hopeful. In their experiment, the pupils were encouraged to read their work and to employ cue cards that used sentences with the type of constructive comment a conversational partner might express. Evaluative statements on the cue cards were, for example,

'People won't see why this is significant', 'This doesn't sound right', 'This is good'. Directing statements used were 'I'd better give another statement', 'I'd better say more', or 'I'd better change the wording'. Pupils using cue cards of these types were able to internalize the process of revision and its purpose.

Conclusion

All these approaches aimed at supporting pupils' writing can be developed in the primary classroom to positive effect. Research is useful in the way that it provides insight and helps teachers focus on the difficulties that children encounter when writing. Through being able to appreciate the problems, we are in a better position to support progress. Professionally, it is not easy to know exactly how to move a child from the knowledge-telling position of writing shown so well in the following description:

> I have a whole bunch of ideas and write down until my supply of ideas is exhausted. Then I might try to think of more ideas up to the point when you can't get any more ideas that are worth putting down on paper and then I would end it.
>
> (Bereiter and Scardamalia, 1993:160)

Aldous Huxley describes a very different process of knowledge-transforming writing, which is one that allows him to rework his thoughts. He says,

> Generally, I write everything many times over. All my thoughts are second thoughts. And I correct each page a great deal, or rewrite it several times as I go along . . . Things come to me in driblets, and when the driblets come I have to work hard to make them into something coherent.
>
> (1963: 197, cited by Bereiter and Scardamalia, 1993)

It has been shown that the road from conversation to writing in the knowledge-telling model (and there can be many levels of quality and competence within this model too) through to finally knowledge-transforming writing is a hard one for adult, teacher and child! Individuals need to be able to operate both in order to function in a literate society. In the next chapter, we will consider what the child has to become aware of in order to appreciate the difference between the various genres and what she has to know to be able to write appropriately in the different forms for specific purposes.

2

Developing an Awareness of Genre

Granting that children have some kind of awareness of literary forms,
the problem then becomes to explain how this knowledge is brought
into use in writing.

(Bereiter and Scardamalia, 1993:166)

Introduction

In the first chapter, we discussed the route along which the child
passes on her way to being able to express her own thoughts, ideas
and messages as a text. It is a tortuous journey with many hurdles,
pitfalls, twists and turns along it. We addressed the issues involved
in the process of writing, by exploring the difficulties and challenges
that the young writer faces. After dispassionate analysis of what is
incurred in the translation of speech into print, the wonder is not that
some children fail to write either very well or very much, but that so
many find their own way into it, and some by the age of three-and-
a-half years old. It is also amazing that the main or 'big idea', that
writing is concerned with communicating meaning, is within the
grasp of almost all nursery pupils. And, interlocked with this 'big
idea' in children's minds, is the notion that the language and form
that the writing takes depend on the intended communicative purpose of the writer.

Long before formal schooling, children demonstrate an awareness
of purpose and form in writing, when they 'write' a letter to 'Father
Christmas', label a drawing, make a list to go shopping with Dad,
design a card for Gran's birthday, draw a map to show the way to
the shop and compose a story for their action man. There is serious
debate about how and in which direction the next steps should be
taken, and the exact way that primary teachers should support

16

children to take them. Should explicit teaching occur? Or should teachers build unintrusively on this early, intuitive, implicit knowledge about language in a wider sense? (Figure 2.1.)

Genre theory

The 'caught versus taught' debate has, not surprisingly considering the degree of interest in genre theory, generated some heated academic argument. Fuelling the controversy is empirical evidence, which perversely supports both sides. Beginning her own discussion on the matter, Littlefair says 'research enables us to understand more about the varieties of language we all use as we write or speak in different situations for different purposes, and audiences' (1993:128). Here, Littlefair is referring to genre theory, which is a theoretical explanation concerning the generation of texts to fulfil specific, social purposes, for particular audiences, and the consequent need to adhere to the appropriate forms. The theory is based on a functional approach to language, particularly Halliday's work on language (1975, 1978, 1985), which is considered seminal to the formulation of a theory related to the genre of text. In Halliday's view:

- we learn language
- we learn through language
- we learn about language.

Figure 2.1 A reception child's version of the Cinderella story

So the prins danz with eindrel

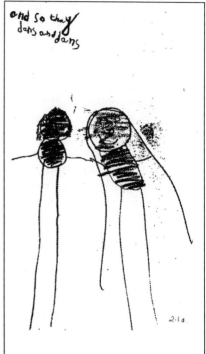

and so thay dans and dans

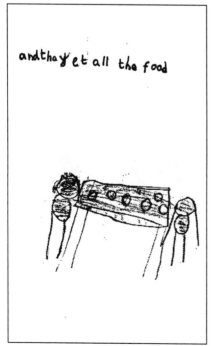

and thay et all the food

and then thay went home and wene thay got home thay went to bed

and the moning came
and cindreL wac up
So did the Prins
and the Prins
Said

Wer am I

Wer am r

I yo bac, no yow do nt

yow cam to stay
Said cindreL
yow cant yo bac

We or yo wing
To yet marid
Said cindre L
so thay yot marid
an thay Livd ba-PLy ev aft

Young children *learn language* by using it. They learn to speak through the innate and seemingly insatiable desire to communicate and to make meaning. Vocabulary is enlarged as new words are needed to express exactly what they want to say. Many thousands of interactions occur before the child is a truly competent language user. In addition, acquaintance and proficiency with written language develops knowledge of spoken language in particular ways.

We also *learn through the medium of language*. We discuss and explore, through interaction with individuals more knowledgeable than ourselves, how the world operates. Questions are asked, concepts and ideas are developed through talking, reading and writing, and our understanding is increased. We learn to name objects and actions and qualities. We learn to organize our representation of experience to ourselves under the tutelage of syntax.

By using language constantly, on a daily, minute-by-minute basis in a vast range of situations, *we learn about language*. Children puzzle out how it works, they formulate the rules of language. Through usage, trial and error, they discover the rules for plurals, for past tenses and how adverbs work. This astonishing and creative linguistic act is demonstrated when young children charmingly over-generalize rules they have self-formulated and produce inventions like 'mouses', 'I see'd' and 'I tried my very bestest'. This knowledge about language is implicit, and the fact that humans learn how to speak by speaking forms the basis of one side of the debate, about whether formal teaching about language should take place in primary school, or whether it is largely unnecessary, or even, as some believe, counter-productive.

Before looking further into this issue, we need to clarify what genre theory is, and whether it concerns only written language.

What constitutes a text?

In common usage, the term 'genre' usually refers to the way that books or films are categorized. Novels are described through literary types, examples of this being 'science fiction', 'detective mystery', 'historical romance', or as one form of genre is now described by television producers as, 'costume drama'. By this is meant the form of historical drama such as the serialization of Thackeray's *Vanity Fair*. But the genre theorists suggest that this commonly held meaning is too narrow a definition and that the term 'text' can usefully be applied to a much wider range of language-based activities. The widening of the definition of genre is supported by also embracing a broad view of what constitutes a text. Kress and Knapp suggest that texts are interactions and are 'produced in response to, and out of, particular social situations and their specific structures' (1992:5). This definition emphasizes the social and cultural features as well as the linguistic, which dictate the production of a text. An elaboration of this notion that genre refers to all linguistic communications was formulated by Martin, Christie and Rothery:

> Genres are referred to as *social processes* because members of a culture interact with each other to achieve them: as *goal-oriented* because they have to get things done; and *staged* because it usually takes more than one step for participants to achieve their goals. (1987:59)

To see how this definition actually operates in real life, look at this example of an exchange in a post office:

> Good morning – lovely day! (*greeting*)
> Yes, isn't it? – It won't last till the weekend – typical! What can I do for you? (*response/conventional query*)
> May I have six stamps, please? (*request*)
> What sort of stamps? (*clarification sought*)
> For postcards to go to Greece. (*supply of information needed*)
> Would you like the special issue ones? How many did you say you wanted? (*further clarification*)

This type of interaction is both highly staged and goal-oriented; the social protocol might vary in different parts of the country or the number of conversational turns taken might be influenced by the length of the queue in the post office. But we all know quite definitely that a long discussion on the probability, according to the law of averages, of a wet weekend versus a fine one is not expected! We know intimately the structure of these social interchanges; our lives are full of them and we know them without explicit instruction. They just appear to happen 'naturally'. It is the recognition of the structure of communication that is at the centre of genre theory and of this volume. Kress suggests that texts have 'a high degree of internal structure' (1982) by which he is referring to the conventions, rules and forms of the interactions. We use a script, in effect, and one which is appropriate. What dictates that structure will now be considered.

The structure of texts

Purpose is the major influence on the structure of a text, as Littlefair says of genre that it is 'a purposeful, communicative activity' (1992:10). She continues, reiterating the link, 'We might say that purpose and genre are almost synonymous' (1993:129). Its intended purpose influences both the features of the whole text, that is the larger structures of the form and style, and also the linguistic features at sentence and word levels. Kinneavy, Cope and Campbell (1976) describe the product, or the result, of the influence of purpose on structure as the 'mode of discourse'. In other words, the structure supports the intended purpose of a text, whether it is spoken or written, in order to make that purpose as clear as possible.

Let us, for example, consider the persuasive genre, or mode of discourse. Some of us are better at constructing an argument in this genre than others. Barristers are probably the most skilled, but we all know children who are impressive. The conventional form to construct an argument is as follows:

The opening remark usually acknowledges that the listener/reader has a point but then several counter-arguments are put forward to make a case or counter-argument, reserving the most convincing for the final statement. We know that too many reasons only confuse the issue and that three or four strong points usually achieve the intended outcome! Most convincing as a 'clincher' is reference to a higher authority such as the law, the school rules or something the receiving participant has said, or allowed to happen, in the past. The structure for both oral and written texts in the argument genre is that of a sequential organization, the chosen order of which is key, for maximum effect. When writing, the points of the argument will be laid out on separate lines for emphasis, even in a formal letter. These conventions can be seen operating in these two texts:

Example 1

Child to parent: I know *why* you say that I can't go to the town hall disco. But it is on Thursday and that's *nearly* the weekend. *All* my friends from school are allowed to go. And, I have done my homework, all of it, and you did say that the charity it's for is a *very* good cause.

Example 2

Dear Gordon

I realise that you have a right to come and go, whenever you please, to your own flat. However, I would like to point out that at 4.00am the rest of the house is trying to sleep.

Most flat owners have to go to work in the day and being disturbed in the middle of the night does not make for good neighbourly relations.

Coming in talking loudly, banging the front door, and then playing music which can be heard in other flats contravenes the lease that you signed when you purchased a flat in this house. The lease states clearly:

'Flat owners are not allowed to make *any noise* in their flat that can be heard outside it, between 11.00pm and 9.00am.'

We would ask, please, if you could be more considerate in this matter.

With good wishes
Alastair and Yvonne

Culture is another determiner of genre. We do not communicate with each other in a vacuum but in a society with culturally constrained and specific ways of interacting. These rules have evolved not only, as we suggested, to make the purpose clearer, but because, by following the conventions, the intention is achieved most effectively. The conventional modes of interacting oil the wheels of human intercourse in a civilized society. The earlier example from the post office showed this well.

The letter above, from the exasperated middle-aged flat owners complaining to a twenty-six-year-old neighbour, who is a clubbing fanatic, is constructed as a factually based, unemotive argument courteously using constrained, non-abusive language. The linguistic style is culturally typical of the generation to which the couple belong, and the message is imbued with sufficient formality which, they hope, will curb the wild excesses of youth! It is culturally driven.

We become more aware of the influence of culture which is highly context-specific and, as we have seen, generation-specific, when we are abroad and different conventions operate. Policemen, shop assistants and restaurateurs have different ways of conducting interactions – an alternative 'modus operandi' makes even mature travellers feel unnerved and unconfident. It becomes apparent in this situation that the structures of interactions are not 'natural' but acquired and culturally rule-bound. A recent experience in a Spanish *venta* demonstrated this, when the owner would not allow an upgrading of the wine which accompanied and was included in the price of the *menu del dia*. Thus by his illogical but custom-driven prohibition he lost some extra profit! The conversational exchange was completely outside our previous experience, in our own culture.

Register is the term that relates to the appropriate choice of language that is made as the result of the situation in which the communication is embedded. Halliday (1978:32) describes register as being concerned with the fact that 'the language we speak or write varies according to the type of situation'. The writer or speaker operates in a context, discusses a certain topic, and usually with an intended audience in mind. Halliday (1989) again is helpful in clarifying these three features of any communicative situation in the following way:

- the *field of discourse* – which is the general area of concern, the subject matter
- the *mode of discourse* – the medium of language, written or spoken, and its internal organisation
- the *tenor of discourse* – the relationship between the participants, the degree of familiarity between them.

To use the example of the letter of complaint again, the topic is sleep being disturbed by a thoughtless neighbour. This is the *field* of discourse. It is written as a non-narrative text with the sequential format in the argument/persuasion genre. The *mode* is written and the discourse has some formality due to the nature of the letter which mimics semi-legalistic language, and which aims to be courteously intimidating in order to achieve its effect. It is relatively formal due also to the age gap between the participants. One *could* simply write 'Why can't you shut up when you come in at night! You selfish git!' And it concludes in a friendly, conciliatory 'we have not taken offence and are still speaking to you' style. This is the *tenor* of discourse, and can be divided further into functional (concerned with social function) and personal (concerned with attitudinal elements) tenor.

Register is how genre is embodied. Of the interrelationship of this and the previous discussion Littlefair summarizes well:

> a writer chooses a genre which is suitable for his or her purpose. The genre form relates to the cultural form of expressing meaning. Genre can be considered as the framework of a written or spoken communication. The writer expresses details of the communication in a register of language which is inevitably constrained by the immediate situation. (1993:131)

The different types of written genre

Given the vast extent and range of purpose that written texts address, it can be imagined that a list of genres will not be exhaustive. However, in a volume purporting to encourage children's understanding of and ability to use different genres in their writing, it behoves us to search for a broad agreement on a workable list of the different types of genre.

Theorists vary in the way that different genres are categorized.

Collerson (1988) separates *early genres* (labels, observational comment, recount and narratives) and *factual genres* (procedures, reports, explanations, and argument or exposition). Wing Jan (1991) suggests that texts can be divided into *factual genres*: reports, explanations, procedures, persuasive writing, interviews, surveys, descriptions, biographies, recounts and narrative information; and *fictional genres*: traditional and contemporary modern fiction.

Lewis and Wray (1995) in their book use the main list of non-fiction genre generated by the Australian theorists, Martin and Rothery (1980, 1981 and 1986), whose ideas were further developed by Callagan and Rothery (1988) and Macken *et al.* (1989). Macken *et al.* collected and analysed examples of children's writing and from this, the research team identified six main types of non-fiction genre, which are:

- recount
- report
- procedure
- explanation
- persuasion
- discussion.

Believing as we do that a strong case can be made for the place of narrative fiction in the young child's life and in the curriculum, we also will discuss and give suggestions for the way that the literary genre can be developed in the writing of young pupils.

The 'caught versus taught' debate

How do children comes to recognize the subtleties and complexities of genre?

Powerful research evidence has confirmed and reaffirmed that young children acquire intuitive understanding about language and its use, and this is demonstrated by their competence, long before formal schooling. We have seen the level of implicit knowledge shown by a young child earlier in this chapter. The dilemma is how to harness this knowledge into a more formalized working grasp of the rules and conventions of the various modes of discourse, and in a way that will support pupils' later learning and advanced thinking. On the issue regarding direct, explicit teaching about the various modes of discourse in the early years classroom, Meek says, 'Whether it is imperative formally to teach the discourse of a subject in the early stages of learning its content is a recurrent discussion among educators' (1996:10).

Nearly fifteen years ago, HMI were recommending that teachers should:

> teach pupils about language, so that they achieve a working knowl-
> edge of its structure and the variety of ways in which meaning is made,
> so that they have a vocabulary for discussing it, so that they can use
> it with greater awareness, and because it is interesting. (DES, 1984:27)

Although HMI do not make it clear whether the directive here refers to explicit teaching, Yetta Goodman (1984) warns that this approach has its pitfalls. She asserts, as have we in Chapter 1, that the development of written language is hugely complicated and when children are given rigid instruction on the mastery of one skill or rule before another, sight is lost of that rich complexity. The activity is in danger of being rendered meaningless. Also with an instructional approach, it is difficult to take into account what the learner already knows.

So perhaps it seems that the most effective route to language learning, for the youngest pupils, is a matter not simply of direct teaching but of a broader range of experience. We would argue that the need is to offer both. Certainly, some researchers would argue that to offer children a wider opportunity is a beginning towards improving matters. Martin, Christie and Rothery are critical of the narrow experience of genres that are provided in the early years of school when they write:

> that children should be stranded there writing stories, for example, as
> their only genre in infant and primary school, is impossible to accept.
> It cuts them off absolutely from any real understanding of what the
> humanities, social sciences and sciences are on about and denies them
> the tools these disciplines have developed to understand the world.
> (1994:237)

Kress is also convinced that access to a broad range of genre is essential, but suggests no direction as to the route that this should happen. He writes:

> In my view there are genres, they and access to them are unevenly dis-
> tributed in society, along the lines of social structuring. Some genres –
> and the possibility of their use – convey more power than other gen-
> res. As a minimal goal I would wish every writer to have access to all
> powerful genres. This is not the position in our society now. (1987:43)

We, as teachers of early years pupils, believe strongly that the way forward lies in giving children real opportunities and meaningful experiences that will show them clearly both the purpose of and the need for the various modes of discourse. In addition, we wish to promote the kind of teaching that will cultivate their understanding of the distinctiveness of the different genres and so enhance use of the appropriate linguistic structures in their own writing. As Carter argues, life and teaching in a classroom does not have to be an either/or:

> it is wrong to assume that conscious knowledge operates independently of unconscious knowledge; there is constant interplay between different modes of knowing and explicit analytical attention to language can and should serve to deepen intuitions. There is a continuum from intuitions about language, reflection on language and analysis of language, recursive and mutually informing. (1990:18)

This is our stance as authors and we seek to describe how to build upon intuitive knowledge in order to make explicit to the child herself what she already knows and so to deepen her understanding and thinking, and in so doing make possible the use of language to meet her own needs and the demands of school learning. In later chapters, we will make suggestions as to the way that this might be achieved with writing in the different genres, but first let us consider the complementary processes of reading and writing.

Reading non-fiction texts

Reading and writing are closely related, if not the exact mirror-images of each other, as we saw in Chapter 1. They each have influence on the development of the other, writing being concerned with the encoding of speech into print and reading with the decoding. One provides essential insight into the working of the other. It therefore can be argued that children will learn a great deal about the distinctive nature of the various types of genre through reading and using texts for their own purposes. Whilst the non-narrative book presents a different type of challenge to the reading skills of young readers, Littlefair (1993) believes that teachers' sure knowledge of genre and register provides them with the linguistic tools with which to examine the texts used in their classrooms, and serves to enhance their understanding of why, when and where children will need support.

The *National Literacy Strategy Framework for Teaching*, with its recommendation that both 'shared' and 'guided' reading should include the frequent use of non-fiction books, has resulted in the more common appearance of high quality reference texts in early years classrooms. Publishers have responded by producing enlarged versions, for 'shared' reading, of interesting and well-produced examples of books of this genre.

Difference in structural organization of text

Non-narrative texts of all types demand different approaches to reading. Firstly, non-fiction books are rarely used sequentially, from start to finish, in the way that a narrative is read. Readers dip in and out, go back and forth, sample and seek the information needed. Secondly, the format of the page presents directional complications in that the print does not always follow the left-hand corner to right directional pattern, line by line, and with a 'sweep back' organizational format. Thirdly, information is presented jointly in text supplemented with diagrams, photographs, tables and maps, all of which require a quite different type of literacy in order to access the information. The term for this kind of reading is *graphic literacy*.

Conceptual issues

Information texts are only useful if the reader has sufficient knowledge of the subject area to be able to make sense of what is offered. This close match of a book to the child's developing understanding requires careful monitoring by the teacher – too great a gap frustrates a reader to the point of demoralization. Information texts also contain a much higher proportion of content words than fiction, often with a specialist vocabulary. These words need to be understood if the text as a whole is to fulfil its purpose. The use of an index can be valuable here although with very young readers this is not straightforward. Probably more helpful is a preparatory discussion before reading, or a 'rich introduction', by the teacher, of the type recommended by Marie Clay in her Reading Recovery Programme, and now taken up by the National Literacy Strategy for 'guided' reading.

We will now consider the particular challenges that different kinds of non-narrative books present to children.

Expository texts

This type of book is probably the most utilized non-narrative text in primary schools. The term 'expository' covers the genres of exploration, description, persuasion and argument. Young readers find the register of the language the most difficult of all the non-narrative category of books. Not only is the text arranged differently from narrative, which usually has a chronological order of events, but the content is concerned with abstract notions that deal with the building of an argument such as relating cause and effect, distinguishing problem and solution and comparing and contrasting concepts.

Another potential difficulty is the complex grammar used by the authors of these texts; for instance, the way that the sentences are linked and the particular kind of cohesive ties used which are distinctive to the genre. In addition, in order to achieve a more objective stance, the passive voice is frequently used. Longer sentences with several clauses and sub-clauses are yet another feature of expository texts.

This impersonal language is the language of formal documents and business and it represents the highest status linguistic mode of communication of our society. Children need to become familiar with the way that it operates in order both to have access to and, eventually, to be able to use it for their own purposes. Littlefair argues that 'Many readers who are able to read simply structured text probably require further help so that they can read complex written expression' (1993:134). Donaldson gives the reason why teachers should support their pupils' mastery in reading of the non-narrative genre when she says:

> They need now to enlarge their understandings of the many ways in which words can be handled with skill on the printed page – handled to achieve economy, or elegance, or emphasis, or surprise, or cohesion between sentences, or logical clarity in a sustained argument, to name only a few of the aims that concern an author. (1993:54)

A tall order for early years children, the teaching of whom is the focus for this book! But it is important that their teachers have a clear idea of their aims, the ultimate goal of which is to support children to be able to read *and* write in the knowledge-transforming mode which we discussed in the last chapter. With the aim of helping pupils understand the different structure, syntax and register of non-narrative texts, we introduce children to a writer's purpose and consequent choice of appropriate language.

Procedural writing

Because of the problems that expository texts present to children, many non-narrative books are written in the procedural genres. Publishers find that through listing information and writing instructions, many of the inherent grammatical complexities, encountered in expositionary texts, can be avoided. Science books are often written in this mode, with observation and experiment activities presented in a type of 'recipe' formula. This can make for wearisome reading with the didactic 'Take a bicycle pump and two rubber bands' formulaic presentation of content, but after the appropriate explanation from an adult, pupils are able to seek out and use the information.

Linking reading back to writing non-narrative texts

Given that we are concerned with writing in this book, it is interesting that Littlefair suggests that 'Perhaps the clearest way to familiarise children with the construction of non-narrative text is for them to write and discuss their own information texts' (1993:137) and this is what we intend to do. She goes on to say that if pupils are to become competent readers and writers of both narrative and non-narrative genres they must be:

> able to discover information and reconstruct it for their own purposes. . . they require a sense of the overall forms of these genres and of the language which is commonly used. (1993:138)

3

Teaching the Early Stages of Learning to Write

I think that there is at least one belief that all of them (the researchers) would share; the belief that children are highly active and efficient learners, competent enquirers, eager to understand.

(Donaldson, 1993:36)

Introduction

Evidence from research carried out over the last two decades into the thinking and learning of very young children led Donaldson to make this often quoted and truly apt statement. Her faith in the extraordinary capacity of children to wonder, to ponder, to hypothesize in order to make sense of their world and its systems, was substantiated through her own long acquaintance with the cognitive abilities of preschoolers (for example, 1978). In addition, Donaldson cites the work of Wells (1985a, 1985b), Tizard and Hughes (1984) and Hughes (1986), all of whom reaffirm the competence of children to acquire spoken language before school, and to begin to get to grips with the complex number, graphic and written language communication systems of our society.

Spoken and written language development

The toddler learns to speak, certainly without direct instruction, but through a powerful desire to communicate meaning. She both learns *how* to use spoken language, and learns *through* spoken language about her world (see Chapters 1 and 2). The child is supported in this formidable endeavour by adults who encourage her conversational attempts, who make it worth her effort by signalling comprehension and also by repeating and extending the utterances in positive rein-

31

forcement. By the time the child enters school, she has a vocabulary of between 5,000 and 30,000 words and generally has mastered most of the grammatical structures necessary to make known her needs and wants.

The pre-school child's extraordinary capacity is directed towards working out written language, too. Literacy is 'parasitic' (Bielby, 1999) on spoken language in that generic competencies of making meaning through a symbolic system are employed afresh in learning the new mode of language. And in so doing, spoken language development also progresses. The phase between about six months and school entry is considered to be one in which the child is in the process of becoming literate, and this period is termed the 'emergent literacy' phase. The term was first used by Marie Clay (1966) when, through her own work into 'concepts about print' for her doctoral thesis, she brought to the attention of educationalists her view that children, in the developed world, are never 'pre-literate', in the sense that they are completely oblivious of or untainted by print. But rather, they are slowly working out a written language system, through many, many different personal encounters with text, books and stories, almost from birth.

Embraced within this notion of emergent literacy is also the idea that young children get to grips with print through the twin activities of reading and writing. We discussed this view and the interrelatedness of decoding and encoding in the previous two chapters. We suggested how the complementary processes of reading and writing develop alongside and mutually inform each other, with writing as the productive language mode progressing more slowly than the receptive (but also active) mode of reading. The two modes of written language cannot be separated either conceptually or practically. On this Clay says:

> A theory emerges which hypothesizes that out of early reading and writing experiences the young learner creates a network of competencies which power subsequent independent literacy learning. It is the theory of generic learning, that is, learning which generates further learning. The generic competencies are constructed by the learner as he works on many kinds of information coming from the printed page in reading or going from the printed page in writing. (1991:1)

Ferreiro and Teberosky (1982) go further on this interrelationship, by emphasizing the link more strongly through the notion of complementarity. They describe the process of writing as the child getting to grips with the alphabetic code in a self-instructing, positive and active way, as she works at the encoding of her thoughts, ideas and speech, and as a result, pushes forward her decoding abilities.

What is known about the experiences that provide these pre-school opportunities to learn about literacy?

Research into the emergent literacy phase

The work of both cognitive and experimental psychologists, as well as of those engaged in ethnographic research, has identified and confirmed that there are fundamental understandings the child needs to acquire on the path to literacy:

- the links between speech and writing
- the unchanging nature and communicative function of text
- the conventions of the print system.

Upon these foundations, the pre-schooler is able to acquire:

- an understanding of the alphabet as a code.

This research has been described by many writers (e.g. Riley, 1999) and the scope, space and intention of this volume preclude great detail here. The experiences that seem to facilitate these understandings that are 'the seed corn of the child's fascination with print' (Riley, 1996) occur, as happened earlier with learning to speak, in the home environment (this work is usefully summarized by Sulzby and Teale, 1991).

In the home, the learners are able to practise the language systems, both spoken and written, through interactions with others in a personal, secure and very specific cultural context. Children begin to learn about reading and writing in their homes and within their communities through observing and participating in *culturally situated* literacy practices (Ferreiro and Teberosky, 1982). Research in the 1980s advanced discussion on the type of home that appears to fulfil the 'induction-into-print' role best and insightful work was disseminated (e.g. Heath, 1982).

The 1990s have added to our knowledge, through recent studies concerned with the home-based reading and writing practices that are related to different socio-economic cultures. Given that literacy is not a unitary construct, this concern is extended also to interest in which kind of home environment appears to support which type of understanding about literacy. Purcell-Gates (1996) carried out a study designed to clarify the nature of different emphases placed by various communities on particular literacy practices. We now know that literacy practices differ between communities in a variety of dimensions and it is recognized that the child's pre-school experience profoundly influences success at school (Dyson, 1989; Riley, 1995a, 1995b).

Several studies from the USA have documented that whilst literacy is integral to the lives of both high and lower socio-economic groups, the experiences, and therefore what the children make of them, differ. The lower socio-economic groups continue to achieve lower levels of literacy skill, once at school, than the children from higher income groups. It has been assumed that this is due to different levels of parental education which, in turn, affects the nature and complexity of the literacy activities at home.

One interesting study into the lives of five low-SES (socio-economic status) families whose children *were* successful in school was made by Taylor and Dorsey-Gaines (1988). These children were observed sharing in story and Bible reading events, and they saw their parents reading newspapers and magazines and also writing to various social service agencies and to schools; thus indicating that a wide range of literacy activities in these homes occurred and were educative for the children.

Investigations into the types of literacy experiences

Further studies looked at and separated out the dimensions of various home literacy environments. The research projects aimed to quantify the ways in which the differing dimensions influence the type of knowledge of written language acquired by the child. The identified literacy experiences to which children are party are:

- interacting with adults in writing and reading situations
- exploring print on their own
- observing adults modelling literate behaviours (e.g. reading instructions/writing lists).

Purcell-Gates (1996) through detailed observations in the homes of lower SES families indeed confirmed a varied range of literacy activities. The types of literacy event that the children are likely to share are the following:

- daily living routines, e.g. shopping, cooking, paying bills, etc.
- entertainment, e.g. reading a novel, doing a crossword, reading a TV programme, reading rules for a game
- school – related activity, e.g. letters from school to home, homework, playing school

- work, e.g. literacy used in order to secure or maintain a job
- religion, e.g. Bible reading or study, Sunday School activities
- interpersonal communication, e.g. sending cards, writing and reading letters
- story reading.

In addition, the texts used by the adults were analysed for the linguistic complexity at vocabulary, sentence and clause levels. Purcell-Gates found that there was considerable variation in the quality of the print experiences to which the children were exposed and this she attributed to different levels of the *functional literacy* present in the twenty families studied. This was clearly related, as has been suggested by the earlier studies, to the educational level of the adults. In these lower SES families the most frequently observed print event was literacy being used in the domains of *entertainment* and *daily living routines*. The rich data make compulsive reading as the fabric of the daily lives of these families emerge from the journal pages.

Where the study advanced thinking from that of the 1980s was by using an innovative methodology in which the researchers linked the home literacy experiences of the child to her knowledge of written language. This was an attempt to unravel the connections between pre-school experience and success with literacy once at school.

The main issue for the purpose of this chapter is that it would seem that homes at all levels of socio-economic status and education offer many and varied opportunities for children to develop understanding about spoken and written language. What appears to differ is the quality of the encounters and the extent to which they are capitalized upon by the adults. We suggest, therefore, for teachers of early years pupils to make pre-judgements about the ways in which pupils will approach the task of literacy once at school, on the basis of their socio-economic status and the educational level of parents, is both risky and foolish. What seems to make the difference is the child's transactional stance to learning, that is, her ability to make sense of the learning opportunities offered by school and the extent to which these are built on the home experience. This, in turn, is affected by the teacher's ability to assess the child's prior knowledge of literacy at school entry and thus to be able to provide well-matched learning activities. This is a point that will be developed later in the chapter.

Story book reading and parent teaching

Another study (Senechal *et al.*, 1998) attempted both to quantify and differentiate between the particular contributions that the reading of stories and the direct teaching of pre-school children make to the level of success, once at school, with their oral and written language skills. The findings from other studies and this are that:

> parents distinguish between two different kinds of experiences with print at home. Some experiences provide more informal or implicit interactions with print such as when parents read to the child. In this kind of experience, children are exposed to written language, but print *per se* is not the focus of interactions. Other experiences provide more formal or explicit interactions with print such as when parents teach about reading and writing words and letters.
>
> (Senechal *et al.*,1998:109)

The distinction between the informal and the formal is whether the focus of the experience offered the child is on the message contained *in* the print or whether it is *about* the print itself. The Senechal *et al.* study (1998) indicates that the different kinds of literacy experiences are related to the development of different kinds of literacy-related skills. The distinction appears to be between the development of the 'big picture' about literacy and a more focused print or alphabetic knowledge. The former should not be lost in the pursuit of the latter. Certainly, there is a need for more research to be done with greater numbers of children at all levels of the socio-economic scale, but at a basic level this work is revealing to teachers that children learn, not so surprisingly, from the experiences they are exposed to and what they are taught. Whilst children are skilful at making sense of situations for themselves, if their attention is explicitly drawn to aspects of literacy, then that is what, inevitably, they will focus upon. It would seem wise to suggest that young children are given broad, balanced and meaningful experiences with written language in order that they will also develop their 'transactional stance to learning' and so be successful at school. As we suggested earlier, they need first and foremost to become aware of the purpose of print, its rules and conventions, and this should not be sacrificed for too focused a teaching of print and its detailed features.

Making marks

McNaughton *et al.* (1996) describe a New Zealand study that looked specifically at the writing of children. The study was designed with a Vygotskian perspective that proposes that the child 'co-constructs' her understandings of literacy through interaction between her own mental constructs and society (in this case her own family's influence). The work has echoes with the research findings of the previous section, but moves our argument on further. This theory has six propositions (McNaughton, 1995):

1. *Families arrange time and provide resources which socialize children into their practices of literacy.* Adults read to children, take them to the library, newsagents and bookshops and supply felt-tip pens, pencils, crayons and chalks for children to mark–make.

2. *Family literacy practices reflect and build social and cultural identities.* As we saw from the North American work described before, children see their parents carrying out many different types of literacy activity. These are culturally specific in the sense that the activities have different emphases: in some families filling out football coupons is common, for others completing crossword puzzles is an occurrence most often watched by children. In some homes, adults using word processors may feature prominently, whilst in others, as in the McNaughton study, letter writing is a frequent occurrence as in Samoan families separated from each other by great distances.

3. *Literacy practices are expressed in specific activities, such as goals, rules and ways of carrying out this activity.* Both reading and writing practices are shared and modelled in a variety of ways. For example, books are read straight through, or they are talked about, or perhaps used as a vehicle for teaching and labelling objects. Writing is an activity which is meaningful and for a purpose or a dull lesson on letter shape, a 'fantasy trip or a meaningless exercise' (Smith and Elley, 1998).

4. *Two basic and complementary types of learning systems occur, and each can be expressed in a number of ways.* On the one hand pre-schoolers are given assistance, 'tutorial support' in their early writing attempts, and on the other the child works at her own puzzling out of the code system.

5. *What children learn to do with written language is become experts within particular activities.* In one home a child will become good at labelling, another making lists, yet another writing notes for individuals. This has implications for the educational setting in which the pupil finds herself at the stage of school entry.

6. *Development is enhanced by the degree to which settings are well co-ordinated in terms of practices, activities and systems of learning and development.* This last proposition has implications for both the nursery settings and sensitive dovetailing of teaching; and also for the desirability of reception class teachers becoming fully aware of the extensive and personal prior learning of each pupil.

Research into the transition from school to home

Going to mainstream school presents the child with many challenges and discontinuities. Bennett and Kell (1989) show that there is a great deal with the potential to confuse and bewilder the new school entrant, such as the physical environment, the school routines, the language used by the adults and the learning experiences offered. This is before considering the effect of separation from the adult emotionally closest to the child for longer periods than previously experienced.

There is also evidence regarding the continuity in literacy learning that going to 'big school' threat to entails. Baker and Raban (1991) found that one child regressed after entry into reception class in her confidence and willingness to work on her own understandings with print. Anecdotally, Benjamin, in our first chapter, a pre-school message and letter producer, lost his sense of purpose and belief that he could write after entry to school. Another large-scale study (Riley, 1996) showed that children arrive at school with a wide range of rich but highly idiosyncratic knowledge about literacy, and the extent to which teachers capitalized on these understandings and enabled the children to progress, through appropriate teaching and matched activities, varied hugely.

McNaughton's findings were in tune with these studies. Nineteen children, from eighteen families across three ethnic groups, were followed for a chronological year, six months before starting and six months after school entry. All the children produced large amounts of writing using a variety of genres. The most common category was labelling, and that was chiefly putting names on drawings. Narrative was the next type of writing most frequently seen by the researchers. Exposition and argument were seen much more commonly at home than when the children were at school. This consisted of explanations of how games worked, diagrams for models and such like. On arrival at their three respective schools, two groups of the children produced twice as much writing as they had prior to starting school, whilst one group produced considerably less. We will now consider which practices at school build on pre-school knowledge and competence most effectively.

Approaches to teaching writing

Large numbers of children enter school as eager learners and writers, and leave it as reluctant writers.

(Hood, 1995, cited by Smith and Elley, 1998:36)

The fourth of McNaughton's propositions suggests that there are two modes of learning that operate together: firstly, the child working on her own understandings, fathoming out the alphabetic code system for herself, and secondly, the child being supported, *when necessary*, by an experienced language user. This dual-pronged effort is amazingly powerful and is noted by many of the researchers into this phase of development. This is true of both learning to read and learning to write. As we have said before:

> Two important features emerge from this body of work into the emergent literacy phase. Firstly, the research findings view the child as an active contributor to her own learning. This learner-centred view of the pre-school reader and writer is greatly influenced by Piaget, Bruner and Chomsky, each of whom see the child as being a constructive, hypothesis-testing, rule-generating agent in her own learning. Secondly, the studies cited highlight the role of the supportive, interested, interactive adult, who 'scaffolds' the child into greater understanding. These two crucial aspects of the literacy learning have implications for the following phase of development.
>
> (Riley, 1996:8)

Studies confirm the value of teachers being accepting and, therefore, able to capitalize on all that has been learned by children before school (Berwick-Emms, 1989; Riley, 1995a). Teaching in the nursery and the first year of school needs to be undertaken with great sensitivity, in order that prior and valuable learning is not ignored or, worse, cut across, so that the child's own active approach to learning is not undermined. The pupil needs to continue to believe in her own abilities as a problem-solving language learner for sound and sure development to continue.

In McNaughton's study cited earlier, two interventions were undertaken with the class teachers. In the first intervention, the researchers took into school the portfolio of work completed by the children before school, but the teachers, whilst interested in it, seemed to make little diagnostic use of it. In the second, workbooks for use at home were initiated as a means of bridging the home/school literacy divide. These the teachers did use positively as a source of information on the child's level of functioning in a different context.

We believe, with Carter, that 'conscious knowledge' operates in union with the 'unconscious' and that, indeed, 'there is constant interplay between the different modes of knowing' (1990:18). This is a challenge for a teacher with thirty or so children in her care and, with the current DfEE exhortations to whole-class teach and so follow the stipulations of the *National Literacy Strategy Framework for Teaching* (DfEE, 1998), can seem to run counter to this principle of supported but autonomous learning.

Implications for practice

It may be that certain types of pedagogy are taken from the NLS *Framework* for specific reasons, whilst we recognize that there is a place for a variety of methods and approaches, that can and should be used in early years classrooms. The various approaches will support different aspects of the writing process and promote learning behaviours and styles that are crucial for the development of literacy.

A clear distinction must be made between the teaching of compositional skills and the teaching of transcriptional skills for very young children. Writing is too complex an activity for attention to be focused on all aspects of the process simultaneously. Teachers are wise to plan for the regular and systematic teaching and practice of the transcriptional skill of handwriting, including copying and tracing, which should be taught on a separate occasion from one with a focus on composition. Also, alongside the learning of the correct formation of letters, the practice and reinforcement of the names and sounds of the letters can occur.

Planning for the teaching of writing

All primary schools will have a policy which provides information on the progressive teaching of different skills and aspects of writing such as genre, presented as schemes of work or *long-term plans*. These are now hugely affected by the NLS *Framework for Teaching*, with its term-by-term teaching objectives for each year group, from reception to Year 6. *Medium-term plans* develop from the above, and can be thought of in terms of the three types identified by SCAA (1995b), namely 'blocked', 'linked' and 'continuous':

- blocked planning refers to a discrete unit of work, such as to focus and teach all Year 1 classes on the beginnings and ends of stories in narrative fiction writing over a period of three weeks
- linked planning might link English teaching to other curriculum areas; for example, to strengthen the understanding and use of report writing through specific science work
- continuous planning provides for the on-going routines of usually skill-based work which should occur regularly and frequently, such as the teaching of punctuation.

Short-term plans are expanded from the medium-term plans, and also provide discrimination between pupils with different learning needs through differentiation in the learning activities offered.

Provision for self-initiated writing

Planning for the teaching of literacy in any early years classroom will include planning for child-directed opportunities to read and write, encompassed within the learning environment. Teachers will be aware of the value of a well-resourced, designated area for writing, with furniture and materials arranged in just such an inviting way that encourages the pre-school kind of self-initiated experimentation and active learning. Writing areas will vary in emphasis between a nursery setting and a Year 2 class, but much will remain constant. The physical location of this space will have been carefully considered and often will be placed near the quieter reading/listening area, and certainly as far away as possible from the construction and art resources work spaces.

The resources in a writing area

Space will dictate the lavishness of the provision, from an area that consists of several square metres and is semi-partitioned, with wall displays (of alphabet charts, handwriting and calligraphy examples, spelling lists of keywords, days of the week, months of the year, starting points for writing), shelving, stationery racks, books, dictionaries, encyclopaedias, and thesauruses, and at least one computer with word processing packages. Alternatively, in very cramped conditions, the writing area might consist simply of one piece of display boarding with a table placed in front on which the resources are laid. Resources, also, will vary according to space, school, class ethos and finance. The following resources are essential:

- pencils (with different grades of graphite), pens, felt-tip pens, crayons (pencil and wax) and highlighter pens
- paper of various types, quality (including rough paper), pre-cut in different sizes and colours
- various pieces of card as above
- ready-made blank books of various sizes and colours from mini-books to A4
- envelopes and notepaper (even own class-designed headed notepaper)
- blank greetings cards (also class made as above) and envelopes
- blank official forms (e.g. clothes catalogue forms)
- examples of address books, birthday books and diaries

- clipboards, bulldog clips, paper clips, staplers
- erasers, pencil sharpeners, glue-sticks, sellotape, masking tape, scissors, trimmer
- handwriting cards, books, guidelines.

The following resources might be included from time to time:

- book-making materials (pre-cut paper, needles, thread, bookbinding tape, appropriate types of glue)
- boards and material for book covers
- loose-leaf folders
- calligraphy materials, charts and books, stencils, Letraset
- post-box
- boards and chalks
- shallow trays with sand for letter formation tracing
- notice board or message board
- easel with A3 paper
- displays of poetry and story writing
- bins of alphabet books.

Role play areas that encourage writing

Traditionally, early years settings have encouraged independent writing through role play and this should continue, capitalizing as it does on the child's pre-school positive learning stance. Nursery and reception classes provide:

- home corners with telephones, message/list pads, notepaper and envelopes
- shops of various kinds with posters and price lists of merchandise and bills
- hospital corners/baby clinics with patient progress cards and prescription pads
- cafés with menus, order pads.

Year 1 and 2 classrooms provide role play areas such as:

- offices with computers, 'photocopiers', stationery of all kinds, and dictation pads
- estate agents
- travel agents
- opticians
- vet surgeries
- hairdressing salons
- airports and aircraft flight decks.

All of the above specialist areas demand writing of a particular 'genre', for a specific purpose or audience, and on specialist stationery designed for an appropriate use. Teachers have a role here too, in the way that they are able to model how best to use the area and its resources. A teacher joining in the dramatic action strengthens the involvement of the pupils and also demonstrates the expert literacy user during the play; for example, writing a letter to the Big Bad Wolf complaining about his misdemeanours.

It is worth mentioning in this section the current concern about the level of boys' literacy, which appears to be lower than girls, right from baseline entry through to GCSE. Boys tend to use writing areas less than girls (QCA, 1998) but respond well to the more activity-oriented role play areas and where writing is seen to be fulfilling a genuine purpose. It behoves teachers to take care and effort throughout the early years of education, to motivate boys and to encourage them to consider that writing is a valuable and necessary skill to perfect. It is in these years that enduring attitudes, both positive and negative, to writing are formed.

Writing after reading stories or in drama

Writing can follow the reading of a story naturally and with great pleasure, or it can be included as part of a drama. Year 2 children can act out the story of the *The Three Little Pigs*, writing to seek planning permission for their various houses, by using appropriate sample letters such as those in *The Jolly Postman* by the Ahlbergs (1986).

The Literacy Hour

The National Literacy Strategy expects teachers to provide reading and writing learning experiences for children at *word, sentence* and *text* level, for a daily minimum of one hour. The NLS stipulates that the literacy teaching is also to be offered through three different ways of working or approaches, which are: *shared, guided* and *independent* reading and writing.

The *Framework for Teaching* sets out the format of the Literacy Hour very clearly so it is unnecessary to do so here, but rather we will discuss the benefits and shortcomings of the approaches, in order that teachers are able to determine for themselves when an approach is likely to serve their intended learning objectives and teaching purposes. As indicated earlier, we believe that additional time, outside and beyond the Literacy Hour, will need to be provided for certain opportunities for effective teaching of writing to occur. This might be considered when planning for continuous or linked teaching objectives.

Shared writing

Shared writing has its roots in both New Zealand and North American traditions. Don Holdaway (1979), in the first of the two countries, developed 'shared reading' that had the same qualities of the shared bedtime story, of supporting the young child's early reading attempts in a way that 'scaffolds' understanding and makes explicit to the young reader what she knows already, in order for further progress to be achieved. Techniques such as using familiar, often repeated texts coupled with interactive teaching were also commonplace in this approach to reading, from which shared writing is considered to have developed.

Complementary to this approach, Donald Graves (1983) in the USA proposes a process approach to the teaching of writing, in which the pupil is given a constructive role as an active learner developing hypotheses about the nature of language and the writing process through her own writing. In this approach, errors provide opportunity for insight into the text and print processing that the child is able to achieve. This again is in line with the thinking behind miscue analysis (Goodman, 1973) and running reading records (Clay, 1993). The key concepts of the process approach to writing are:

1. *Ownership.* Writing is a demanding and challenging task. In order to assure the high level of motivation which is required to overcome the taxing nature of the task, Graves suggests that children should be allowed to choose their own topic for a great deal of the time in early years classrooms.

2. *Drafts and revision.* Writing is seen as evolving, not arriving perfectly formed on the page with the first draft. Through revision, writers have the chance to operate the deeper mechanisms of the writing process and allow the advancement of ideas to be pursued through a reworking of text (see the Hayes and Flower model in Chapter 1).

3. *Conferencing.* This is the aspect in the Graves model where most of the teaching takes place. The teacher provides an audience and gives feedback to the writer, thus the writers receive clarification, and in so doing the difficulty of one of the most challenging aspects of writing is solved – namely, the conceptual problem of writing

for and putting oneself into the position of an unknown audience. With this mode of teaching, a particular aspect of writing can be focused upon and explicit help and advice offered.

4. *Publishing.* This important feature of the process approach provides purpose, motivation and feedback by making the product available to others. Importance is vested in the presentation of the product which is offered for public recognition (or criticism?).

Implicit in the Graves approach to writing is the *modelling of writing* by the teacher and for pupils. This modelling is the basic principle behind shared writing. The teacher demonstrates to children what experienced writers do, the mechanics of what has to be undertaken for a text to be constructed. In the earliest stages of learning to write, the adult will show, first, how the planning is done, and then on to operating within the conventions of print, and to working out the sound/symbol system of a particular word. Children are introduced to the challenges of writing and how to solve them, as well as the delights and satisfactions.

Shared writing can be used with benefit with all age groups in the primary school, with the whole group or with smaller groups, and is an approach we demonstrate in the later chapters. In nursery and reception classes the reworking of a favourite, well-known tale is a supportive way to reinforce the structure of narrative at both text and sentence level. This approach is well used by teachers with texts such as 'Would you rather?' (Burningham, 1978). A pre-written 'Would you rather your Mum and Dad . . .' can be offered for the children to supply the most stomach-churning, embarrassing suggestion that they can think of, in place of Burningham's original 'had a row in a cafe?'.

In Years 1 and 2 the modelling can include and make explicit the planning stage of writing with the adult thinking aloud, 'I wonder how we should start our story?', 'What, then, shall we make happen?' and so on to 'How can we end our story? . . . is that surprising enough? . . . do we want everything to end in such a straightforward way? . . . could we think of an unexpected twist for the end? . . . like in such and such book we read?'

As Washtell (1998) says, shared writing can be used to demonstrate:

- a sense of purpose and audience: voice (formal or informal); planning; drafting; revising; proofreading; presentation (publication)
- content and features of different types of texts: linguistic features; structural features; vocabulary choices for specific genre; grammatical features
- transcriptional skills: punctuation; spelling; handwriting

- self-help strategies: correcting mistakes; discussing; peer conferencing; collaborating.

Guided writing

Guided writing is the counterpart to guided reading, when focused teaching occurs with small groups of children who are at similar levels of literacy ability. Examples of teaching that can be accomplished with guided writing through the early years are:

- In the reception class – teachers may choose to support the development of grapheme/phoneme association through writing. This is a clear example of the way that the two processes of reading and writing promote progress of each other. We have written before (Riley, 1996:88) on this approach to develop reading through enabling children to hear and identify the constituent sounds in words, then map those sounds onto letters and groups of letters.
- In Year 1 – the teacher scribing for the group their own jointly constructed, dictated story, thus releasing pupils from the burden of transcription. The mirror image version of this activity is when the teacher dictates a story to the group of children to write and so, conversely, they are freed of the task of composition.
- In Year 2 – collaborative writing: children are set an activity, the purpose of which is to support mutually the writing of each member of the group. The task might be first to sequence, to write an outline (composed of brief sentences) and then to rework a known story by fleshing out the outline plot. This activity rehearses the narrative structure by using a well-known story, practises sequencing, and then provides, through collaboration, support with the transcriptional skills of spelling, paragraphs and punctuation.

Independent writing, its development and support, will be discussed in the next chapter.

4

From the First Marks to Writing for a Purpose

Let us accept that those children, when they write, make an approximate correspondence between sounds and letters. They may face orthography problems, but they do not have any further problems with writing, because they are now functioning inside the alphabet system of writing.

(Ferreiro, 1985:84)

Introduction

The previous three chapters have discussed the intellectual task that writing presents to the child. Firstly, children have to understand conceptually the nature of literacy or the 'big picture' and what it offers individuals. Secondly, there is the knowledge connected to the translation from spoken language into written language and what that entails; involved in this also is the close relationship between reading and writing. We addressed earlier the way that each mode of language informs the development of the other.

Encompassed within this second understanding are the layers of awareness gradually acquired by the child, one of which is of the alphabetic code as a system that enables the encoding of the sounds of speech into print. This chapter will focus on the development of these two aspects of writing, and the way that understanding of the alphabet system develops *through* the child writing texts in order to fulfil a variety of purposes. In other words, the writer uses text to fulfil certain purposes and in order to communicate these purposes in written language she needs to work out the code system, alongside the conventions and forms for the various genres. We will argue that *genuine* understanding of the nature of the alphabetic code only develops as the child both decodes and encodes texts. Appropriate direct teaching that supports emerging understanding is crucial, but the child initially has to make the connections for herself through her active experimentation with mark-making.

Interaction with a range of texts

Chapter 2 cited the research evidence confirming the learning about literacy that occurs in the home environment long before children enter school. Stories and books are enjoyed from a few months old, and as the emergent literacy phase progresses the child becomes increasingly knowledgeable and discriminating about print and so becomes nearer to being able to read conventionally as entry to school approaches. The awareness of print, its purpose and conventions occurs through observing people write and also through making, for herself, different types of text. Whilst narrative is the most common and memorable text that babies and pre-schoolers encounter, they do become closely acquainted also with a range of other kinds of texts. Very early books are often not stories but of the 'picture and caption' category, and the texts that children see produced at home are virtually never narrative. Pre-schoolers are more likely to observe their parents and carers writing shopping lists, notes to other people, letters and cards; children see adults completing forms, football coupons and paying bills. As a result, children's early attempts at writing are most frequently in the non-fiction genre and many of these show a primitive awareness of purpose influencing both the form and the language of a text.

Early mark-making

The sensual joy of leaving one's mark is essentially human. Food is swirled into patterns with fingers, bubble bath foam is trailed across the side of a bath. As soon as they are able to hold an implement, children make more permanent marks on surfaces with lipsticks, felt pens, pencils, sticks or paint brushes. Toddlers are undiscriminating about the surface – walls, table tops, mirrors, bedspreads, floors, sides of boxes, paths of soil or sand, and occasionally even paper, are all equally satisfactory and satisfying. Experimentation with this vigour and on this scale with this flexibility seems to be universal once an implement presents itself and role models of mark-makers are available. The ability to represent the world through this mark-making becomes more refined as the child becomes able to articulate her intention. It is at this stage that the mark-makers demonstrate that they have acquired the concept of literacy, which is shown through their dawning recognition of the difference between writing and drawing.

Figures 4.1 and 4.2 show that both these very young children are clear about what they have made: Benjamin has made a drawing and Sean has 'written' a communication. At three years old, Benjamin continues to build on his idea of the distinction between drawing and writing by signing the picture he drew while on holiday (Figure 4.3). The child's name is of crucial importance to the emergent awareness of both self and literacy. The link between name and identity makes the written form of particular interest to the child, and is often the focus of the early teaching of letters by parents and carers. Thus their name is usually the first word that can be formed by children and the letters of their name then begin to appear frequently, if randomly, in their independent attempts. The 'ability to write own name' used as a measure at school entry was the second most powerful predictor of early success in reading in a study of the literacy progress of 191 children through their first year of school (Riley, 1996). In that study, it is argued that if a child comes to school already able to write her name, it denotes a deeper conceptual understanding of literacy and the alphabet system.

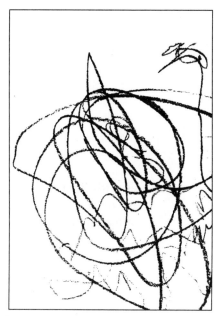
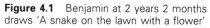
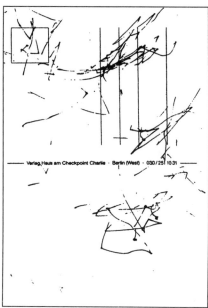

Figure 4.1 Benjamin at 2 years 2 months draws 'A snake on the lawn with a flower'

Figure 4.2 Sean at 2 years 'writes' a card to his Grandma whilst on holiday

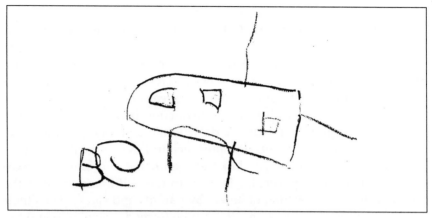

Figure 4.3   Benjamin at three years 'signs' his picture

But at four years and six months old, in the quotation at the beginning of this book, Benjamin is stoutly maintaining that he is *not* able to write. One might argue that he is demonstrating that he has the concept of literacy firmly established because he 'knows what he does not know'! Following that statement, though, together we achieved the text reproduced in Figure 4.4.

Figure 4.4   Roy, I am sorry you didn't come to see me

The conversation that preceded the text went like this:

JLR: Of *course* you can write!
Benjamin: Can't.
JLR: Well! I bet you can . . . let's see . . . where do you start writing?

Benjamin made the huge dot at the top left-hand corner in true infant-instructed style to remind him of the direction of written English.

JLR: Now, what are you going to say to Roy?
Benjamin: Well! I wanted him to come too.
JLR: Great . . . he'll be pleased to know that . . . so how shall we actually say that?
Benjamin: Roy . . .
JLR: Fine . . . off you go then . . . what does Roy begin with? Can you hear the sound? yes 'rrr' that's good . . . now what's next?
Benjamin: 'oy' . . . how do I write that?
JLR: It's actually two letters though it doesn't sound like it . . . it's 'O' and a 'Y' . . . like at the end of 'toy' and 'boy'. OK what are you going to say next?
Benjamin: 'I am sorry . . .'
JLR: Right then, off you go . . . 'I' . . .

And he was away . . . Benjamin knows a lot more about writing than he realizes, he knows the conventions of print, the left-to-right directionality of text and the sweep back from the right-hand end of the line onto the next line (left-hand end). He is aware of the fact that there are spaces between words, thus indicating that he can identify a word, with some support, as a unit of meaning. On receiving help with phonemic segmentation, he can map the units of sound onto a symbol (or symbols), once it was separated and identified as distinct from the other constituent sounds in the words. His mapping is more or less accurate, and when not, it is logical. Because he can read quite well he knows his letters and the sounds they make. Also, as stated in Chapter 1, he copies under his teacher's writing every day, and after six months in school his motor control and actual formation of letters are fairly good. The handicap to Benjamin's development is that in his class situation, he has not had the experience of writing to fulfil his own purposes nor has he experimented by himself with his growing understanding of the alphabet code.

Composition and transcription

This code awareness aspect of writing is referred to as spelling with older children and as a transcriptional skill it is contrasted with our earlier preoccupation with composition in Chapters 1, 2 and 3. However, with very young children the distinction between these two aspects to writing is not clear-cut. The ability to express oneself is dependent upon the ability to master the alphabetic code, or at least, to have worked out the main principles of how to translate spoken language into written text. In this section, we are deliberately ignoring the role of formal teaching at the moment for two reasons. Firstly, the child is usually in the home or nursery environment at this stage of literacy development and the majority of the learning occurs through seeing literacy in operation around her. Teaching, at the very most, will be in the form of appropriate, sensitive and judicious intervention. Secondly, the immense intellectual leap of being able to 'function in the alphabetic system' (Ferreiro, 1985) can only be achieved if the child actively engages with literacy in order to develop her own understanding.

Finding their way into the code system of writing

Given opportunity and encouragement young literacy learners progress a great distance on their own. Research evidence (Clay, 1975; Ferreiro and Teberosky, 1982; Bissex, 1980) suggests that this exploration is not only helpful but essential. Clay (1987), following her study on early writing, suggests 'I doubt whether there is a fixed sequence through which all children must pass. The path to progress is likely to be different for different children' (cited in Smith and Elley, 1998:120). However, stages of development related to spelling or the understanding of the alphabetic code have been proposed (albeit on a sample of one!) and are a useful guide to early years teachers.

Gentry (1981) identified developmental spelling stages:

1. *Pre-communicative*
Characteristics:

- the child knows the difference between drawing and writing, that symbols create a message and have meaning
- the writer at this stage often invents symbols, in addition to using a range from several literacies such as logos, numbers, letters, frequently from her own name, and is unconcerned whether they are upper or lower case
- she makes no connection between sound and symbol.

2. *Semi-phonetic*
Characteristics:

- the child is beginning to link letters with their sounds (grapheme–phoneme association)
- knows how writing is arranged on the page, and has a primitive understanding of form
- although knows word boundaries, often words are abbreviated (and the vowel sound omitted)
- recourse to earlier use of invented symbols on occasions.

It is important to recognize that no stage is absolute and that children move between them.

3. *Phonetic*
Characteristics:

- the child is able to discriminate the sounds in words and map them onto symbols consistently, although they may violate accepted letter patterns of English, e.g. monstr (monster), ate (eight), fort (thought)
- builds a sight vocabulary of known words.

4. *Transitional*
Characteristics:

- the writer is able to move beyond relying solely on the sound–symbol correspondence principle and begins to be able to appreciate the accepted spelling patterns (strings) of English. This means that children are able to process print in orthographic chunks (Frith, 1985), rather than letter by letter conversion only. This is due to a developing visual memory and is related to the stage of reading development.

5. *Correct*
Characteristics:

The child has a basic knowledge of spelling strategies which are demonstrated by:

- the use of visual strategies
- an understanding of the basic spelling patterns of English (i.e. the rules and systems)
- a knowledge of word structure – morphology

- the ability to distinguish between homonyms (to *row* a boat, to have a *row* with someone) and homophones (*bare, bear*)
- growing control over the spelling of loan words (e.g. *pajamas* as pyjamas).

Examples of children's writing

In the following examples the children demonstrate these different spelling stages alongside a developing awareness of genre, as they experiment with and use writing for a purpose.

Pre-communicative stage

- Uses writing-like symbols to represent written language.
- Assigns a message to own symbols.
- Uses known letters or approximations of letters.
- Is aware print carries a message.

Alice's letter (Figure 4.5) exhibits all the features of this stage.

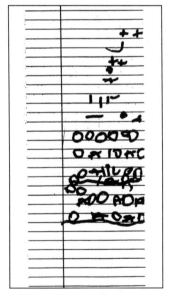

Figure 4.5. Alice's letter

There are letters (O, A and i) and letter-like symbols (+ and - for example). These are repeated frequently but there is no evidence that they are linked to sound in any way. Clay (1975) suggests that there are a number of principles that children adhere to before they understand the spelling system. They are:

- the recurring principle: this refers to repeated marks.
- the flexibility principle: this refers to the invention of letters – the knowledge of letters leads to experimentation.
- the line and page principles: directionality – left/right and top/bottom, etc.
- sign-concept: awareness that print carries meaning.

All these principles are demonstrated in Alice's letter, together with an additional one of:

- form principle: that different purposes for writing require different ways of overall representation on the page.

This last principle is shown by the form of the communication in that it is a letter. Whilst the author's intention is to communicate, the message remains locked in the marks and is 'pre-communicative'. What is fascinating about this piece is the aspects of the conventional letter form it takes. Alice has noticed the 'shape' of a letter and incorporated this into her writing. It begins with four short lines placed on the right-hand side. She may not know that this usually represents the correspondent's address, but has noticed that writing at the beginning of a letter appears in this way. The main part of the letter has lines of symbols which fill the lines across the page. Finally there is her signature at the bottom.

Semi-phonetic stage

- Uses left to right and top to bottom directionality.
- Relies heavily on the most obvious sounds in words.
- Represents a whole word with one, two or three letters.
- Uses mainly consonants.

Rebecca, four-and-a-half, in Figure 4.6, is just moving from the pre-communicative stage into semi-phonetic. She was asked to draw her family and she has attempted some rudimentary labelling. She knows where to attach a label and has made a sound/symbol connection with Natalie and Mummy. Rebecca uses the initial letter, representing the most important sound of each of their names. Those letters are placed next to the appropriate drawings indicating a developing understanding of where labels are placed on pictures.

Tanya, four-and-a-half years old, when invited to do the same task, has made a drawing of her family and friends (thus including 'significant others') more like the list that it is logically (Figure 4.7). What is noteworthy here is the distinction that is made between the two

Figure 4.6.   Dad, Natalie, Mummy and Rebecca

Figure 4.7.   Tanya's family and friends

groups of people. The first row represents her family and the second row of people are her friends. Thus she has drawn on several literacies to contextualize herself in diagrammatic form:

- categorization
- the use of pictures to help the reader

- the two categories demonstrate that she wishes to represent the important people who are a distinctly different group from her immediate family.

Assad, seven years old, has written a non-chronological report in memory of his trip to the park (Figure 4.8) which clearly shows the indicators stated above. He is operating in a language that is additional to his mother tongue and is chronologically older than generally is the case for this stage of writing.

Phonetic stage

- Chooses letters on the basis of sound.
- Represents all the essential sounds of a word.

Tanya, now three and a half months older than when making the original representation of her family, has made great progress (Figure 4.10). She knows word boundaries, each spoken word is represented, she has a developing sight vocabulary: *my, Tanya, and, is, Nabhah, got*. Her grapheme/phoneme attempts are logical: *cold/called, sesta /sister, inthe/ another, lev/live, wth/with*. Linguistically, Tanya has

Figure 4.8. Assad's trip to the park   **Figure 4.9**

Figure 4.9.   My name is Tanya and I've got a sister . . .

written with a straightforward and unproblematic use of language, appropriate to the recount genre.

Another example is Figure 4.9.

In Figure 4.11, a six-year-old compiled a list of things one must do and eat in order to remain healthy. This demonstrates a child solidly in the phonetic stage but with an element of the next, the transitional stage. There are many examples where the child is choosing letters purely on the basis of the sounds of the word-maker's East London accent (e.g. exasisin = exercising). However, there are also some words which demonstrate common letter patterns and their use in a variety of words (e.g. teeth, sleep) even if they are then over-generalized, as with 'cleen'.

Transitional stage

- Uses common English letter sequences when attempting unfamiliar words.
- Uses letters to represent all vowel and consonant sounds in a word, placing vowels in every syllable.
- Is beginning to use visual strategies (e.g. common letter patterns).

Ben has also made a list (Figure 4.12), this time of his favourite things to eat, to remind his Dad when he goes shopping. It shows a child of nearly six years old slightly more advanced than the previous boy. The list format has been adhered to again. More words are spelled

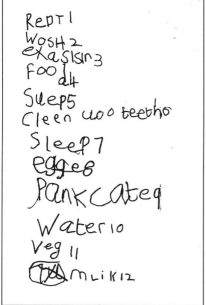

Figure 4.11. List of things for healthy living

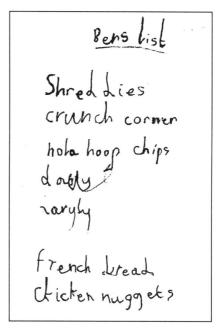

Figure 4.12. Ben's list of favourite foods

accurately with a good use of visual memory for the conventional spelling patterns.

Lily, five-and-a-half years old at the end of her Reception Year, is showing her developing understanding of both the alphabetic code through her spelling and the narrative genre (Figure 4.13). She does this by the following:

- her use of the time-honoured literary opening 'Once upon a time'
- setting the scene with the main character, the snail – who was slower than all others and who wanted some friends
- developing the narrative through the refusal of several creatures to be his friend – the tension builds.

Lily is showing understanding of the elements of story (see Chapter 5).

Each of the above examples demonstrates not only the children's increasing control over the alphabetic system but also significant understandings of the conventional features of each distinct form. Just as teachers need to build on and develop the technical aspects of letter formation and spelling knowledge, so they also need to develop awareness of the appropriate structures and the characteristic lin-

Figure 4.13. The Tale of a Snail

Figure 4.13.   (Continued)

guistic features of the different types of writing, clearly linking form to purpose. This teaching is the focus for the following four chapters.

Class contexts for writing in a range of forms

Teachers need to provide the children in their classes with opportunities and reasons for writing using a variety of forms. A rich context would be to create a newsagent's shop in the imaginative play area. This will enable pupils to explore the range of forms and functions of information texts. Initially, a few typical texts from a newsagent's can be brought in and discussed with the children. These might be:

- a newspaper
- a sweet carton
- a receipt
- a video box
- a birthday card.

Children typically know the purpose of each of these items from a long acquaintanceship and show extensive knowledge about them. The teacher might ask the following questions about the text to focus thinking:

- What is it? What is the text for?
- Why do you read it?
- Do we know who wrote it?

Then the pupils' attention can be brought to some of the text features of each example. For example, if the greetings card is examined, what does the information on the front indicate:

- What type of greeting is the card offering?
- What is the age of the intended recipient?
- What do we know about the relationship between the sender and recipient? For instance, is it jokey, casual or formal? Is it male to female, or vice versa? Is it a loving relationship with a close family member or is it professional?

Inside the card the function and grammatical form of the printed message brings another layer of discourse to the card.

A visit to a local newsagent might be organized in order to discover more about the types of texts to be found there. This could involve writing a shopping list beforehand, and so reinforcing the purpose, an aid to memory, as well as the form.

After the visit, children could then be encouraged to stock their own newsagent's in the classroom. They might conduct a brainstorm to decide on the contents they wish to create and then, having had their attention drawn to the different forms, can independently begin the tasks. The contents are likely to include a variety of the following: greetings cards, sweet boxes, invitations, comics, newspapers, notices and advertisements (of the type usually found in the shop windows) and video covers. Children can also be involved in the writing of shopping lists before going to play in the class shop.

Through examples of this type with the potential to engage children with a real purpose, they will be encouraged and motivated to produce a variety of different types of writing showing how much they know not only about spelling and letter formation, and the relationship between purpose and structure, but also about the forms of writing. We will now consider the different genres separately.

5

Writing Narrative Fiction

Storytelling is something we all do and understand. The habit is so deeply sunk in us, historically and culturally, that we recognize our common humanity in all the tales we tell and hear, from childhood to old age, waking and dreaming. (Meek, 1996:22)

Introduction

The early writing of pre-school children involves efforts to label, to write messages and to recount their daily happenings, which then expands into story writing. However, the type of writing that is most frequently experienced by pre-school children is the narrative fiction form and it is this that children tend to engage with at home, both before and after going to school. We should not be surprised at this, since storying, as Meek suggests above, is a psychological necessity for all human beings. Wells (1987), also, is clear about the role of storying in meeting a fundamental need in all individuals.

The structure of narrative fiction

The work of the genre theorists, Martin and Rothery (1980, 1981, 1986), began with a survey investigating the various and most common types of writing found in Australian primary schools. They reported that in the early years pupils initially write in the 'observation/comment' genre, typically a picture with a caption. This 'I went to Mcdonald's and I liked it' type of writing becomes extended with a further string of observations, which are usually elicited by the teacher!

As Martin argues, these texts are highly school-context dependent, rarely appearing outside writing lessons, and they reflect teachers' deeply held views on the child's need to base writing on her own experience and feelings and the necessity to establish ownership of her own writing. The example of Alice (Figure 5.1) demonstrates clearly this form of writing. It was the beginning of the autumn term, and the children in her Reception class had been asked to draw a picture and to write about it, based on an event from their summer holidays. Alice states, 'I went to the water park'. She is asked by the adult how she felt about it. Alice replies that she had a lot of fun and is asked to write that too. Finally, the teacher translates with a conventional transcript underneath Alice's emergent attempts.

This 'observation/comment' form is taught and practised in school from the earliest opportunity, although it is not a common form outside early years classrooms, except perhaps on holiday postcards. However, it is more common in speech. Martin and Rothery suggest that two generic forms develop from this observation/ comment writing. These forms are the recount and the report. It is the recount which provides the foundations for the development of

Figure 5.1. Alice (4.4) demonstrates a typical example of 'observation/comment' genre

the narrative fiction genre, and is the basis for our discussion which follows.

The recount

Initially, the recount is typified by sequences of events, ordered chronologically and connected with 'and then'. Children produce innumerable examples of this form when they write their 'news' on endless Monday mornings, or following an educational visit. Quite why the school visit is accompanied, in primary schools, by a request to write an account of their day out remains a mystery, as usually the description of a child vomiting on the coach is the most interesting and vivid part of the writing! To be fair to primary teachers, this practice might be justified as one that allows reflection on and organization of an earlier experience, although the reality often falls short of the intended learning outcome.

Typically, the structure for these recounts is:

orientation ——————— sequence of events ————————— final orientation

Writing of this type often *begins* like this:

On Thursday we went to the farm. We got on the coach outside school.

Continues with an outline of the *events* of the day:

We saw goats and sheep and pigs and then the cows being milked. Then we had our lunch.

And *ends* with the final event and possibly an evaluative comment:

We got back to school and went home. I had fun.

This is still, recognizably, part of the 'observation/comment' genre. The recount develops into a narrative structure, according to Martin and Rothery (1980), drawing on the work of Labov, when, after the initial *orientation*, there is a *disruption* in the sequence of events; a complication which leads to a final *resolution* (followed sometimes by a moral or coda). It is not until children begin to introduce the dramatic action, the complicating event, that recount develops into true narrative.

Other linguists have used more sophisticated models to typify the narrative fiction structure. Longacre (1976), for example, identifies the following elements:

Aperture	The 'once upon a time' type opening
Exposition	Containing the information about setting (time and place) and characters
Inciting moment	The point when the predictable exposition is disrupted and the story gets going
Developing conflict	The plot reaches a point when the confrontation or 'final showdown' becomes inevitable
Denouement	A crucial event occurs that makes the resolution possible
Final suspense	Details of the resolution are worked out
Conclusion	Some sort of satisfactory end is worked out

Longacre proposes that all these elements are present in stories although some parts of the story may have a dual or even triple function.

We intend to use the three-part model (orientation, disruption, resolution) outlined by Martin and Rothery (1980) for the discussion that follows. We suggest that having an explicit knowledge of the structure of narrative helps teachers to be clearer in their understanding of how to teach children to write stories.

One of the most interesting findings of Martin and Rothery was that although the teachers surveyed in Australia claimed that they placed great store on the writing of 'stories', no pure examples of writing in the narrative form were to be found in the classrooms before the third year of schooling, as opposed to observation/comment or straight sequences of events. While the teachers stated that many opportunities were given to write narrative, the resulting 'stories' contained no evidence of the crucial move to describing a dramatic disruption of the on-going events which leads to a final resolution. It may have been that the teachers were using the term 'chronological writing' as synonymous with narrative. Another explanation may be that the children had not been explicitly taught the features of plot distinctive to narrative. So the pupils had been left to arrive at these understandings through their own reading and the occasional teacher comment such as, 'How did the boy get away from the lion, then?'

We can, however, teach children to distinguish between personal narrative in recounts and reports (which can lead to expository writing) and stories (personal or fictional) which have plots. As we shall show in this chapter, if children both have the story structure explicitly demonstrated, when stories are told and read, and are taught the structure and the process of composition, they *are* able to write in the true narrative form. And often they can do so before they have mastered the technicalities of the English spelling system and letter formation, e.g. Emma's story in Chapter 4.

Despite the somewhat contradictory nature of the survey, Martin, in particular, questions the dominance of narrative reading and writing in the primary classroom. He argues that this domination has significant social consequences. Firstly, pupils' experience of forms of expository writing is very limited, although such forms are highly valued in other curriculum areas, particularly as children grow older. Secondly, this situation disempowers pupils because narrative does not enable them to master the kind of writing that is needed in order to take control of their lives. 'It imprisons them in a world of fantasy and make believe which their society deems appropriate for sub-adults' (Martin, 1984, cited by Czerniewska, 1992:133).

Why teach narrative?

In our view, Martin's dismissal of narrative with the argument that fiction cuts people off from understanding and controlling their own lives is overstated and inaccurate. Taken to its extreme it could be seen as arguing for the exclusion of narrative from the reading and writing curriculum of schools. And yet other linguists, psychologists and psychotherapists take precisely the opposite view. Many believe passionately that stories are the most important means by which individuals come to know the world and their place within it. Barbara Hardy (1977:12–13) puts it this way:

> Narrative, like lyric or dance, is not to be regarded as an aesthetic invention by artists to control, manipulate and order experience, but as a primary act of mind transferred from art to inner life. Inner and outer story telling plays a major role in our sleeping and waking lives. We dream in narrative, remember, anticipate, hope, despair, believe, doubt, plan, revise, criticise, construct, gossip, learn, hate and love by narrative. In order really to live, we make up stories about others and ourselves, about the personal and the social past and future.

The key phrase for us is 'a primary act of mind transferred from art to inner life'. Storying is the human way of making sense, and the better we are at making stories, the more equipped we are to understand and make experience meaningful. It is not merely desirable, it is a psychological necessity. We, therefore, as teachers need to support children in order that they construct their own narratives.

More mundanely, the teaching of narrative is central to our statutory framework for teaching, whether it is the Programmes of Study in the English National Curriculum (DFE 1995) or the *National Literacy Strategy Framework for Teaching* (DfEE 1998). The Cox Committee in its rationale for the original English National Curriculum was clear about the importance of narrative:

> Young children hear stories either told or read from a very early age and, as soon as they have the skill, they read themselves. In this way, they internalise the elements of story structure – the opening, setting, character, events and resolution. Similarly, they come to realise that, in satisfying, well-structured stories, things that are lost will be found, problems will be solved, and mysteries will be explained and so on. (DES, 1989: para. 17.28)

The case for narrative having a major place in the curriculum is a powerful one. The point should be not to imply that we should remove it, as Martin appears to be suggesting, but that narrative should be balanced more equitably with other forms of writing (including poetry, which always seems to be a poor relation). In addition, narrative should continue to have a major place in the later years of schooling and not be marginalized by the other, currently more valued, forms of expository writing that students are required to produce.

As we have stated earlier, we would like to argue that narrative needs actively to be *taught* to young children. In support of this, Christie (1994) reiterates the point that schools fail to show pupils explicitly the nature of each genre, including narrative, leaving children to infer it for themselves through the few clues given by teachers in their general instructions. One of the main contributory factors to this state of affairs is that often teachers are not clear enough about the structures of the genres that they are teaching and therefore are unlikely to be able to make the specific components explicit to pupils.

The development of narrative understanding

Mere narrative becomes story when it has a plot and when it is fleshed out with characters and a setting. The plot is the structuring in a story that faces a character (or characters) with a problem or challenge that has to be answered through action to bring the story to a conclusion, where the problem or challenge is resolved. Characters and settings need to be specified to establish individuals whom we can feel for, in contexts that make the action comprehensible. They provide the concrete terms with which our imaginations can work on.

Given that the component parts of narrative are plot structure, character and setting, what are the expectations of children when they write stories, by the age of seven, for instance? The level descriptors in the National Curriculum for English are as follows:

Level 2 (the level pupils are expected to reach by the end of Key Stage 1): Pupils' writing creates meaning in ... narrative form;

Level 3 (in advance of the expectations of pupils at the end of Key Stage 1): The main features of different forms of writing are used appropriately, beginning to be adapted to different readers.

Explicit references to story structure were excised, wrongly in our view, from the revised level descriptors in 1995, and replaced by general comments about the structure of different types of writing.

From these rather general statements, it can be inferred that children's stories should exhibit simple plot structure to achieve Level 2. In order to achieve Level 3, pupils must in addition make clear reference to characters and setting with some indication that vocabulary and content is being adapted for different readers, for example, for younger children.

These statements are not very helpful as a developmental sequence outlining the characteristics of children writing, showing increased control and understanding of the narrative form. Foggin (1991) has compiled a more detailed hierarchy, which outlines development in terms of structure, vocabulary and the creation and manipulation of character. The insight that Foggin provides is that narrative 'becomes more complex and more mature as the writer becomes more imaginatively interested in the characters (as opposed to the events) in the narrative and, at the same time, becomes more intuitively aware of the needs of the reader' (1991:14).

Foggin suggests the following developmental sequence from reception class through to the age of 11 (end of Key Stage 2):

1. *A main clause plus a list of objects.*

e.g. 'It is my birthday and I got ...'

2. *A list of events.* This is marked by a heavy use of connectives such as *and, so, then, but*. These also typify the markers of oral narrative, according to Foggin.

e.g. 'The boy went to the house and looked in the window and saw a monster so he went home.'

3. *Events causally linked, i.e. plot.* The markers for this kind of narrative are words such as *because, although, when, where, since*.

e.g. 'The boy went to the house because it was raining and he was getting wet. When he got there he looked through the window and saw a nasty monster. He was scared, but talked to the monster. They became friends so he took the monster home for tea.'

In order to develop to the next stage, Foggin states that 'as meanings become more explicit, events will be dramatized'. The next level, then, is:

4. *Story or plot events dramatized*, which includes:

- establishing a landscape or context
- the developing use of dialogue
- other ways of establishing character such as description of appearance
- the development of precise and appropriate vocabulary.

e.g. 'The small boy ran hurriedly through the rain which was soaking through his thin jumper. As he passed the ramshackle mansion he suddenly decided to take shelter there. As he tripped and slid on the entrance tiling, the words of his mother came into his head, "You'll never amount to anything if you don't take chances." . . .'

In Key Stage 3 (11–14 year-olds), pupils demonstrate more complex and layered meanings through creating stories that:

5.   *Combine inner and outer events.*

6.   *Dramatize inner events.*

7.   *Show reflectiveness and commentary.*

Foggin's developmental sequence clearly outlines the main focus for early years teachers: the development of an understanding of plot through events that are causally linked.

Progress only occurs when events are linked to and built on a firm grasp of narrative structure. Thus the central task of the early years teacher is to ensure that children are aware of and understand plot, and demonstrate this understanding in their written stories. The teaching that we provide needs to focus on enabling children to move from writing a main clause and list of events (with the occasional affective comment) through to events being causally linked. From here pupils can move, in the later primary years, to plot events becoming dramatized and development can continue, in secondary school, on these sure foundations. This is not to say that we neglect the description of character, or the widening of vocabulary and the development of dialogue; we suggest only that, in the early years, establishing an understanding of plot is the main teaching and learning goal. Thus, by the age of seven, children should be able to demonstrate in their writing of stories in relation to plot:

- an orientation or explanation of a situation
- followed by a complicating action
- then a causally linked resolution.

They should also *begin* to show that the events are being dramatized by establishing *character* through a simple description, actions and speech, and a *setting*, as well as the use of some carefully chosen words.

The National Literacy Strategy

The teaching objectives contained in the *National Literacy Strategy Framework for Teaching* (DfEE, 1998) which relate to writing narrative focus on these elements too, although it does not argue for plot to be the explicit focus in the early years, as we have done. However, it does so implicitly, if the relative balance is considered. The objectives lay out in detail a progression from the Reception Year to the end of Year 2. There is significant emphasis on oral re-tellings of known stories, and using insights from reading and discussion of what is read, in children's own written narratives.

The objectives that concern the understanding of the components of strong narrative – plot, character and setting – are extensive. These are developed mainly through reading and discussion. The following examples, drawn from the teaching objectives outlined for the first three years of school, are indicative. In the Reception Year, pupils are 'to be aware of story structures, e.g. actions/reactions, consequences, and the way that they are built on and concluded'. In Year 1, children are to 'identify and discuss characters, e.g. appearance, behaviour, qualities' as well as 'to identify and compare basic story elements, e.g. beginnings and endings in different stories' (Term 2). Pupils must also 'compare and contrast stories in a variety of settings, e.g. space, imaginary lands, animal homes' (Term 3).

Alongside these examples of teaching objectives, there is emphasis on the oral telling and re-telling of familiar stories. These range from the 're-telling to others, recounting the main points in the correct sequence' in the Reception Year, to 'prepare and re-tell stories orally, identifying and using some of the more formal features of story language' in Year 1; and then to 'prepare and re-tell stories individually and through role-play in groups, using dialogue and narrative from the text' in Year 2.

The understandings developed through discussion and the re-telling of stories are intended to be taken and incorporated into the children's own writing, whether collaboratively composed through shared writing with the teacher, or independently in their own stories. Thus the NLS requires teachers in England to teach explicitly the component parts of narrative fiction: plot, structure, character and setting, as well as drawing attention to common themes and the typical language used in written story-telling. What is missing, however, is any rationale for the progression, as articulated by Foggin above, nor is the reason given why narrative *should* have a central place in the primary curriculum.

The strategies for teaching the components of narrative fiction which follow are, we suggest, all effective vehicles through which teachers can meet the requirements of the NLS objectives.

Approaches to teaching narrative structure

The following teaching approaches aim to teach children the component parts of stories. Each component has a particular function, and together they produce a coherent whole and a story worth the telling/reading. All these teaching strategies can happen alongside each other and can be used together to help compose and structure narrative.

Reading and discussing stories

When experienced readers read to the inexperienced, in or out of the classroom, they discuss the story as readers. This may involve reading the title, examining the cover and speculating about the book soon to be read. This is followed by a reading aloud of the story, perhaps interrupted by a few questions asked to clarify meaning about events or character motivation, or making connections between the story and the listeners' own lives. The reading finishes with a closed book, perhaps a sigh of pleasure, some talk about the effect of the book, and on occasions a demand for an immediate re-reading.

Through this activity, much is learnt about the pleasures and mechanisms of reading. How can we capitalize on this in order to show children how to read as a writer, and then to write with themselves as critical readers, using their insights and understandings as they do so? The following examples suggest ways in which we can make story structure explicit and thus aid children's ability to operate within and to manipulate narrative.

Re-telling an oral story

A favourite story, from home or class, can be told to a partner. This may be an extended anecdote or a re-telling of a well-known tale. The sequencing of the activity needs to be carefully managed when introducing re-tellings to children of any age. It has to start with the teacher telling a favourite story, and so modelling/demonstrating the oral tradition. This will need some rehearsal, whether an episode drawn from one's own life, or a folk tale. (A favourite starting point for our personal anecdotes is 'The Worst Telling Off I Ever Had!') Before, during and after the telling of the tale, the teacher needs to offer a running commentary on what is happening, making explicit the content and the different components. For example:

> I'm going to tell you a story. I'm going to start by telling you what it's called and then begin the story by describing where I was and how old I was. This story is called 'The Worst Telling Off I Ever Had'. It begins when I was eight years old, and standing in the kitchen of my home. My Mum was just about to give me the biggest bowl of jelly I had ever seen!
>
> The next part of my story is about the naughty thing that happened . . .
>
> The last part of the story is about how my mum found out, and what she said to me and what happened in the end . . .

Once the story has been re-told, the structure can be made explicit again orally ('Don't forget to begin by telling your partner what your story is called . . .') or the structure can be written as three or four prompts on an easel, which the children are able to refer to when they need, particularly when rehearsing their story with a talk-partner. This process can be repeated when re-telling traditional stories such as fairy tales or favourite stories read at home or in class.

Story maps

A very effective way of helping children to order and to consider the ingredients of narrative is through a story map – a pictorial representation of the story. The most suitable stories are those which involve a movement of characters from one setting to another. Folk tales such as 'Little Red Riding Hood', 'The Gingerbread Man',

'Chicken Licken' and 'The Three Little Pigs' work well in this context. Here is an example of an activity with 'The Gingerbread Man':

Materials needed

- Enlarged text 'big book' version of 'The Gingerbread Man'.
- A large (at least A2 size) sheet of plain paper pinned to easel or flip chart.
- The characters that appear in the book drawn in outline and with their names written on them (i.e. woman, Gingerbread Man, dog, cat, fox, etc.) – these are then cut out and have 'Blu-tak' attached to the reverse side.
- Felt tip pens.

The activity

The children are invited by the teacher to listen to the story of 'The Gingerbread Man' The teacher asks the children to listen carefully, as there will be a discussion of the story after the reading.

After the story is read, the discussion begins with the teacher asking where the story starts. When the children have offered suggestions, the woman's house is drawn in the top left-hand corner of the sheet of plain paper. The discussion continues about which characters appear at the beginning, and one or two children are invited to place the appropriate character in the house.

Then, where does the story end? The river is drawn in the bottom right-hand corner. Between the house and the river, a long winding road is drawn. As the story is re-told and the Gingerbread Man's rhyme chanted, and as each new character is met on the road, it is placed on the story map. Finally, at the end of the re-telling, the Gingerbread Man has travelled the road, met all the characters in turn and been gobbled up by the fox. A final re-telling can take place, where the children take it in turns to tell the next part of the story.

A magnetic board can also be used, with the map drawn and magnets stuck to the back of the 'cut-out' characters so that children can have an opportunity to tell the story independently afterwards.

Other methods

Other ways of using the re-telling of well-known stories to give experience of the structuring of narrative include:

- Re-telling the story individually or in groups, each child taking turns to tell part of the story.
- Focusing on the how the story is constructed, e.g. How does it

begin? What happens in the middle which causes a problem? What is the problem? How does the story end? How does the hero-ine/hero sort out the problem?

- Making a story streamer, folding the paper into three or more sections, drawing scenes in order on the paper and using it to re-tell the story.
- Changing a character – ask the children to re-tell the story with a different main character.

Re-telling a story in writing

Similarly, we can make children more aware of the components of narrative through the collective reading and discussion of written texts and by encouraging them to utilize these understandings in their own written stories. A very powerful strategy for helping children to internalize these features is to read and discuss a text (see above) and then create a different story using the same characters, setting and basic structure.

The following example used, as the starting point, three simple stories about a group of dolphins called *The Dolphin Dream*, *The Dolphin Daytrip* and *The Dolphin Dance*, written and illustrated by Colleen Payne (Blue Banana Books). After reading the stories, the teacher and children talked about the four main characters, the trouble they got into and how the problems were resolved at the end. Each text had eight pages. Because the stories were obviously a series, it was suggested to the children that they might like to add more volumes which could then be read by other children in the class and shared at story time. Other difficulties that the dolphins might get into were discussed and also how these could be sorted out. Thus there was a clear context and support given for:

- orientation (including the characters and the setting)
- complication (i.e. the problem or trouble)
- resolution (i.e. how the complication was sorted out).

Sean (5.6 years of age) wrote this story independently as a result:

the dolphins and the Boy

Oence apon a time in May an a sunny day ther was a Dolphin coking under the sea and she

was a nice dolphin her name was Polly. Then pollys friends came alog seeweed sonar kipper and Bottle nose then Polly fergot She was coking and went to play But wile she was playing

Sheekygerge the shark came and ate her and her friends and a Boy thot it was a swimming

pool he Dievd in and cut open the shRk and Rescud Poll and her Friends.

The End.

Sean has used the structure of the original stories in order to compose his own. He begins with the traditional opening 'once upon a time', the *aperture* in Longacre's typology, and the *orientation* (the Who? What? Why? Where?) follows. Sean begins his story under the sea on a sunny day in May and the main character is a nice dolphin called Polly. Her friends arrive and want to play. Sean has set the scene explicitly taking into account the needs of a reader who is perhaps unfamiliar with the other stories in the series, and therefore may need to know that Polly is a dolphin and is also nice.

The complicating action happens swiftly. Before we know what is happening, Polly and her pals have been gobbled up by Cheeky George the shark (another character that appears in the original stories). The boy, who rather curiously thinks that the sea is a swimming pool (Sean himself is scared of the sea, but not of swimming pools), dives in, cuts open the shark and all the dolphins are saved. The problem has been resolved.

Sean also seems to have drawn on other stories to inspire his own, in addition to writing about the characters and using the structure of the original dolphin stories. The complicating action and final resolution are remarkably like Little Red Riding Hood. The teacher compared Sean's story to the originals, in order to make it explicit how he had constructed his narrative and how he might embed this learning the next time he composes a story. All the essential ingredients are there: plot structure, character and setting. Drawing on existing stories in this way supports children's narrative writing beyond the structuring of the whole text.

Sean is also being helped at other levels. At sentence level, his sentences are grammatically correct, and are appropriate for the written story form, as opposed to the grammar of speech and of stories told orally. He also knows that sentences are different in length and short sentences can be used for effect. So he composes a long first sentence up to 'nice Dolphin' followed by a short one, 'her name was Polly'. This literary technique can be pointed out to children when it appears in their writing and in the writing of others, so that they can consciously reuse it in other story contexts. There are also examples of the cohesive vocabulary that needs to be present in order to make the story more than just a sequence of events, and to make the story a coherent whole: *and, then, but* and *while.*

Shared writing

Reading and discussing published stories as potential writers means analysing what writers do in order to compose. We use existing models to guide our own attempts. Shared writing, discussed in Chapter 3, is another powerful strategy for demonstrating what experienced writers do when constructing/composing stories.

Shared writing removes the physical effort of the writing process, and in consequence, gives children insight and power to compose complex texts. Through talking about the developing text and demonstrating how writers reformulate ideas when writing, the teacher is able to be explicit about the procedures and challenges of each particular genre form. Shared writing of a narrative enables teachers to demonstrate:

- the difference between spoken and written language
- where words go on the page
- the relationship of text to pictures
- narrative structure
- the sequencing of events in the story
- typical phrases/language of narrative and descriptive vocabulary.

Preparing for shared writing

Before starting, have all the materials needed ready to use. Materials required are:

- an easel
- sheets of plain paper (A3 or larger)
- *or* a ready-made blank book fixed to the easel using bulldog clips (a ready-made blank book can be made by folding over some sheets of A2 and sewing them together with dental floss at the fold)
- thick felt tip pens.

If children are to illustrate the shared writing, or redraft or publish each page, ensure that the appropriate materials are ready and close at hand.

Introducing the shared writing

Shared writing always begins with the whole class. In a reception class, D.R. starts by drawing on previous knowledge of stories and wondering what kinds of stories and characters the children like. When engaged in shared writing, to 'wonder' constantly is a strategy for fulfilling the most important function: to encourage and shape the children's ideas about how they might express themselves best, and then how it will be written down, as scribed in front of them in the ready-made book or on paper.

The general consensus was that the class liked stories about animals, so the popular choice was that the main character was going to be a sheep. D.R. wondered if the sheep had a name, but it didn't! The children began to think about the complicating action: what exciting event would happen to this sheep? It was agreed that the sheep would get lost in the forest. As ever, many ideas were expressed and one was selected. This again is an important lesson for children when writing creatively – that many ideas are generated and then a selection has to occur.

Generating the text

The children were then split into five mixed ability groups. Each group took it in turns to help compose a section of the story and to illustrate their pages. This provided opportunity to focus children's attention on the elements of the structure as they worked through the story. All this shaping and teaching was done through the teacher 'wondering'. The development of setting, opening and resolution occurred as the writing occurred. Working with small groups gives the opportunity to emphasize story coherence – the way each section follows from, develops or resolves what has gone before. Re-reading the story is important, so that judgement can be made about whether it makes sense and to ensure that each contribution fits in.

This is how the story went:

p.1
The sheep lived on the farm.

p.2
The sheep jumped over the fence.

p.3
It ran away to the forest.

The story begins with a clear orientation, introducing the main character (p.1), then some events leading up to the complication. Short sentences are used on each page, shaped initially by D.R., but increasingly by children as each page composed is prompted by D.R. asking 'I

p.4
The sheep got lost.

p.5
The sheep met a lion.

p.6
The lion roared.

p.7
The sheep went 'Baaaa' and tried to run away.

p.8
The sheep ran deeper into the forest and jumped in the water.

p.9
It saw a shark.

p.10
The sheep jumped out of the water. The shark went mad.

p.11
The sheep wanted to go home.

p.12
It got a bus.

p.13
The bus driver told him off because animals are not allowed on the bus.

p.14
The sheep walked home.

wonder how we could make the ideas sound like a book?'

The complication.

The complication is developed through a series of obstacles to the desired final resolution (i.e. being 'unlost'; getting home). These obstacles are interspersed with commentary on the sheep's actions and feelings, encouraged by such comments as 'I wonder how the sheep felt about that?'

On page 8 with the offering of the phrase 'deeper into the forest' we spent some time talking about how it is a good way of describing where the sheep was running, and is drawn from stories they have heard/read before. It also has the effect of building atmosphere. The move from a longer sentence to the abruptness of the next, 'It saw a shark', is also very effective.

Beginning of the resolution.

Getting lost can be resolved by getting the bus home, but sometimes unforeseen bureaucratic procedures get in the way.

As the story was written straight into the book, the drafting and redrafting of ideas had to be done orally. Individual ideas were talked through, the most appropriate agreed on and then decisions made about how to write before the actual scribing took place.

As each sentence/page was written, writing conventions at the word and sentence levels, such as directionality, punctuation, spelling and grammar, could be discussed and focused on. These were talked about as 'The Story of the Sheep' was written. The finished book, plus jointly chosen title, had the illustrations pasted in and was then read, and re-read, to the class.

Planning frameworks

The final strategy for helping pupils develop an explicit awareness of the components of narrative is with the use of planning frameworks, before the first draft of the story is written. These planners are a powerful way of focusing attention on the elements needed when composing a story, particularly when children are collaborating.

The first example (Figure 5.2) is of a planner that can, with minor modification, be used all the way through the infant school from Reception to Year 2 (and beyond). This example is taken from the work of Dawes who has done much work on planning frameworks for drafting (Dawes, 1995). These Year 1 children had made passports as part of their topic, and then worked in pairs on a story of a journey. They chose the destination and then planned their story. The frame supports their structuring at the whole-text level and the prompt questions help to plan each part. Discussion with a partner

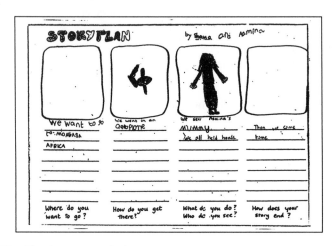

Figure 5.2.   Planning a story of a journey

and teacher provides further support at the sentence and word levels (e.g. 'How can we make that one word "aeroplane" into a sentence so it will sound like a book/story?').

Each pupil then made a little book (Figure 5.3), following the plan but expanding on the writing and elaborating the pictures. Each decided on a title and drew an illustration of herself as author on the back. The teacher interviewed each child and wrote a biographical comment.

The structure of this narrative is an example of a list of elements in Foggin's developmental continuum (see above), although varying the

Figure 5.3.   The book of the story of a journey

questions at the bottom of this planning framework will enable it to be used to support children's construction of the standard narrative plot. For an example, see Figure 5.4.

The next example (Figure 5.5) shows a more complex story planner completed in a mixed Year 2/3 class. This contains more of the

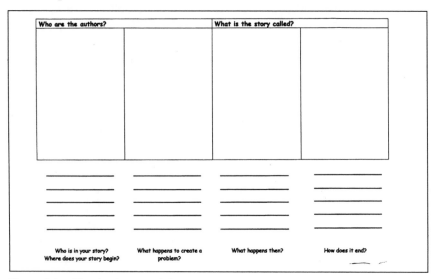

Figure 5.4. Planning framework for standard narrative plot

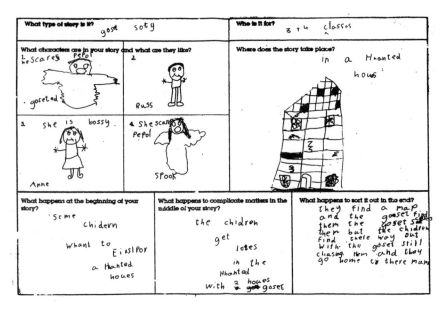

Figure 5.5. More complex story planner

elements that children need to consider. Thus the audience, the characters, with some description, the setting and the plot are all considered through prompt questions.

John and Kim completed their plan after one had been modelled through shared writing. They decided to write a ghost story for the children in a parallel class. They created characters with brief descriptions, although the boy does seem devoid of any personality! There is a single setting (a haunted house), a climax and a resolution. John and Kim then used their plan to compose their story, published it as a little book and placed it in the reading corner of the neighbouring class.

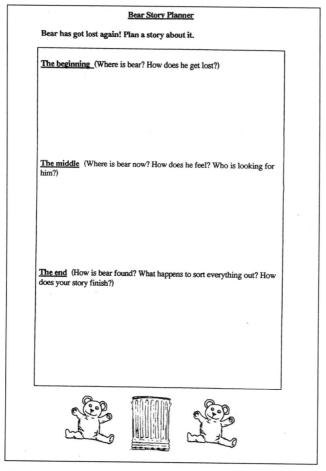

Figure 5.6. Another example of a customized story planner

Conclusion

Planning frameworks are a powerful way of supporting children's developing ability to plan narrative. They:

- focus attention and make explicit the essential components
- provide a framework for thought
- encourage plot coherence
- focus discussion when children collaborate on their writing
- ensure that planning is established as a key component in the process of writing.

In this chapter we have suggested that narrative is essentially typified by variations of the structure:

- orientation
- complication
- resolution.

Children should be taught narrative structure explicitly in the context of:

- discussing stories read
- re-telling known stories
- telling personal anecdotes
- analysing and planning stories using planning frameworks
- composing written stories collaboratively with a more experienced writer
- composing written stories on their own.

6

Writing Poetry

... the best words in the best order, language used with the greatest possible inclusiveness and power. (DES, 1975)

Introduction

RAIN POEM
Frogs in the garden,
Puddles on the pavement,
Rainmacs to keep us dry,
Rainhats on our heads,
Wellington boots on our feet,
Umbrellas to keep our hair dry,
Thunder, lightning and rain all together,
We're happy!
A poem written by 6-year-old children and David Reedy

Young children play with sound patterns, with rhythm and with language. They find both listening to and writing poetry satisfying. Through the influence of poets such as Michael Rosen and Roger McGough, and poetry anthologies collated by people like Morag Styles, the last ten years have seen an increase in the amount of poetry both read and written by children. Whilst not as common as story writing or simple recounts, poetry is an experience that most teachers clearly feel it is essential to offer their pupils.

In this chapter, the intention is to discuss what distinguishes poetry from other forms of text and to suggest classroom strategies that will help pupils to understand the distinctive features of the poetic form in order to help them write their own poetry.

The place of poetry in the curriculum

The genre theorists referred to in the previous chapter are not forth-coming about writing in the poetic form. Perhaps the area is too com-plex for a relatively straightforward structure to be identified (see next part of this chapter for a discussion of this) or perhaps they did not find sufficient poetry, when they researched the different types of writing in primary classrooms, to distinguish it as a separate genre. In addition, the poetic form is sometimes classified as a sub-category of narrative.

Whilst it should not be necessary to justify the inclusion of poetry as an essential part of the English curriculum, this quotation from an HMI report makes the case well:

> Poetry needs to be at the heart of work in English because of the qual-ity of language at work on experience that it offers us. If language becomes separated from moral and emotional life – becomes merely a trail of clichés which neither communicate with nor quicken the mind of the reader – then we run the risk of depriving children of the kind of vital resource of language that poetry provides. (DES, 1988).

This statement is as true for the primary sector of education as it is for the secondary school. Poetry is a unique expression of written lan-guage. To manipulate the sounds and rhythms of language seems to fulfil a fundamental human need from the first months of life. Poetry is a rich language resource in any classroom and, it can also be immensely enjoyable. Poetry builds directly on pupils' earliest and indi-vidual language experience as, from their infancy, children are involved in a culture of songs, rhymes and verbal games. Any observer of young children in the playground will hear them playing with language, learn-ing and chanting rhymes, incorporating snatches of popular song lyrics into their action games and enjoying the subversion of slightly risqué words and subjects. The work of Peter and Iona Opie (e.g. 1959) is a fascinating and encyclopaedic resource on this area.

Poetry or prose?

Any attempt to identify the distinctive features of the poetic form in comparison with, and making it different from, prose encounters dif-ficulties. On this issue, Hull writes:

> For all the strenuous attempts made this century to isolate the poetic by Russian Formalists and others after them, no satisfactory ways of so definitively describing the poem seems to have been reached. (1988:248)

However, the following people have attempted the task:

> Poetry is language used for its deepest and most fully exact purposes.
> (David Holbrook, 1961)

> Poetry is not the study of joy, grief and awe; it is there, disciplined and made accessible by the most sensitive use of the subtlest medium, the native language.
> (Denys Thompson, 1969)

> Someone writes a Poem.
> Poems are constructed, selected, performed, screamed, told, whispered, sung, described, witnessed, seen, felt, and overheard.
> A poem says something.
> Poems are jokes, lessons, games, speeches, complaints, boasts, hopes, dreams, rumours, insults, gossip, memories, lists.
> (Michael Rosen, 1981)
> (cited in *The English Curriculum: Poetry*, ILEA, 1987)

Most of these definitions refer to the power of poetry to depict and record the noblest of human emotions and experience, using 'the best words in the best order'. A daunting prospect for an early years teacher and likely to deter even the most courageous from trying to encourage five-year-olds to write poetry in the classroom! These definitions actually serve mostly to exclude young children's intimate knowledge of the poetic form through nursery rhymes, playground rhymes embedded in 'singing games', and songs, as well as the more general playing with words and sounds. It is precisely this knowledge on which the early years teacher must build.

It seems that the most useful working definition quoted above is that of Michael Rosen. He makes explicit that a poem is consciously designed and composed as a poem. The construction is deliberately a poem and thus there are important decisions concerning the appropriate form, structure and vocabulary. Verse uses the patterns and sounds of language through rhythm and repetition. In addition, a poem communicates a message, which might well be a joke or anecdote rather than a profound comment on human existence. Finally, a poem is written to be read aloud, to come alive in the mouth of the poet.

This definition might, however, equally apply to story as well as poetry. How do we know when a written text is a poem?

W.H. Auden would consider the question to be unnecessary. 'It is a sheer waste of time to look for a definition of the difference between poetry and prose. The distinction between verse and prose is self-evident' (1963:23). It may have been self-evident to Auden, steeped as he was in a lifetime of experience with poetry. Young children, on the other hand, do need to know what counts as a poem. This will invariably happen in the sharing of written and spoken language labelled poetry at home and in the classroom, so that their embryonic understanding of what constitutes a poem develops, as poems are shared again and again. It is the patterning of the language that becomes the key feature to be recognized.

Defining what a poem is, as with all genre, becomes a social activity between writer and reader. If the writer has defined the writing as a poem and wants it to be read as such, then in the classroom the more experienced reader, usually the teacher, concurs with the child and treats it as a text with the distinctive features labelled 'a poem'.

So perhaps we begin to move, slowly and cautiously, towards a more precise definition of a poem. We have suggested that a poem is a highly constructed text, written by a person who defines the writing as poetry. The reader then colludes in this shared understanding and reads the text in a particular way, usually seeking a greater depth of meaning and always seeking the patterning of sound and appropriate rhythm.

The structure of a poem

What are the formal, structural clues which prompt the reader to read a text as a poem rather than prose? How does the label of poem affect the structure? The issue of appropriate structure for a particular form of text is, after all, the central theme of this book! We would argue that poems are, in the vast majority of cases, different from prose in a number of identifiable ways which can be made explicit to children.

The unpublished *Language in The National Curriculum Training Materials* (LINC, 1992b) summarizes the four different areas which we should consider when looking at poetic language and its distinctive features (Figure 6.1):

Sight
Sound
Structure
Sense

Sight

Let us consider *sight* first. Poetry looks different from prose when written on the page; it has a different shape. We recognize the distinctive line breaks (words do not continue to the right-hand margin

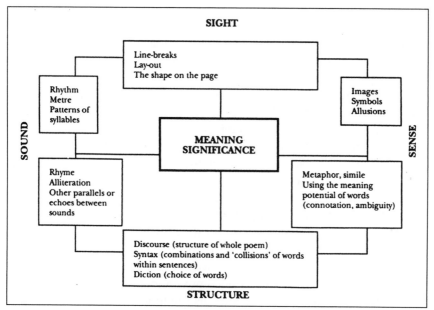

Figure 6.1. Language and meaning in poetry
Source: LINC, 1992b

as they do in prose) and the layout (the poem may be arranged in verses or regular stanzas each containing, perhaps, four lines indicated by a gap between each). This is a clear clue to how we should read the text. This point is well illustrated by Hull (1988). In his example, a pupil, Rachel, has written a response to a film she has seen in the following terms:

> I felt as if something had burst inside of me and trickled into all the parts of my body like a firework going off and sparks sprinkling everywhere.

This reads like prose, albeit with 'poetic language' and use of metaphor. But, Hull suggests, if the words are set out as if it were a poem, this might be the result:

> I felt as if something
> had burst inside of me,
> and trickled
> into all the parts of my body
> like a firework going off,
> and sparks sprinkling everywhere.

The reader is now free to approach the text as if it were a poem, treating the language as more condensed and compressed, and possibly lingering longer over the use of the firework metaphor. Thus at its simplest level, a poem is a poem because we say it is and we recognize the distinctive look of it, and so we read it differently from a piece of prose. There is the expectation of working harder at teasing out greater depth of meaning; there is the anticipation that the poet has used economical and dense language in order to express experience and to comment on the subject matter.

In the above example, there is a change to the structuring of the language, in this case the layout of the text. Lines of text no longer go from one side of the page to the other but are arranged differently; a decision has been made about how many words should constitute a line. In actuality, the problem with trying to define the poetic form and structure is that there is an infinite variety to choose from. If we look at the structure section of Figure 6.1, we see it contains reference to discourse, the structure of the whole poem. There are a large number of distinct structures or poetic conventions to adopt if we wish: we can use well-known forms such as the limerick, sonnet and haiku or have the possibilities of inventing a new discourse structure or rejecting any kind of internal structure and convention in free verse. However, so wide a choice also creates difficulties as well as being liberating.

> The infinite variety of poetic form is one of the great possibilities of the medium, but it also creates problems for children when they write poetry. (ILEA, 1987)

In particular, children need to be introduced to a range of common modes of poetic discourse so that they begin to see what the possibilities are and when to choose to use them for their current purposes. For the youngest children, the problem is even more daunting as they need to negotiate and develop an understanding of how poetry actually is read, in addition to trying to ascertain any cultural significance. This last point begins the discussion on *sound*, in the next section, by acknowledging here that poetry is read differently from prose.

Sound – metre and rhyme

Sound, we would argue, is the crucial feature of poetry, one that can be most readily recognized and which distinguishes it from prose. The *metre* or metrical structure is a significant feature of most poetry. All languages have a natural *rhythm*. Spoken words are made up of syllables. For example, 'one' has one syllable, 'morn/ing' has two syllables, 'oct/o/pus' has three syllables and so on. The *stress* is on one or more of these syllables when speaking. If we say 'morning', we place the stress on the first syllable and say <u>MOR</u>*ning*. We learn these stresses when we learn the language as children. It is a fundamental part of language and almost as important as the words themselves, as it gives spoken language its *patterns* and *cadence*.

Language, composed as it is of stressed and unstressed syllables, is used by the poet who takes these natural rhythms and organizes them in such a way that patterns are formed, consistently and repetitively. This is termed *metre*. When a rhythm becomes standardized through repetition it becomes metre. Poets will select certain types of rhythm depending on the type of poem and the effect that is wanted. Possibly the most well–known metre in English poetry is 'iambic pentameter', where each line of the poem has the pattern of stressed and unstressed syllables repeated five times:

I <u>grant</u> / in<u>deed</u> / that <u>fields</u> / and <u>flocks</u> / have <u>charms</u>
(Stressed syllables underlined.)

There are other types of standardized rhythms, but the formal identification of metre is not the type of complex activity which is best suited to early years classrooms. What is relevant here is the idea that repetitive rhythms are crucial to an understanding of what constitutes the poetic form. This is therefore the most useful focus when teaching the writing of poetry to young children.

Another crucial feature of the sound of poetry is *rhyme*. Of course, one needs immediately to state that poetry does not have to rhyme, even though young children often think that a poem is essentially a set of words which rhyme (which is no more true than saying that all poems have a metre). Rhyme is the repetition of certain sounds, not necessarily related to spellings, often at regular intervals, typically at the ends of lines of poetry. It is important to clarify here that poetry without any formal metre is called *free verse* and poetry without any rhyme but with a metrical structure is called *blank verse*.

As with metre, there are many different conventions for organizing rhymes, which are not relevant to the current discussion. What is relevant is that young children need to appreciate that rhymes exist and be taught how to hear them, to identify them and to generate them if they are to come to know another of the distinctive features of poetry and to be able to incorporate them into their own poems. In addition, the ability to detect rhyme has been shown to have a positive effect on the development of phonological awareness, a necessary skill in learning to read (Bradley and Bryant, 1985). Of course, children need to know that when communicating thoughts and feelings in poetic form it is not necessary for the words to rhyme, and that rhyme is only one of the possibilities to be considered.

The basic building blocks to which the attention of young children should be drawn are:

- the lineation and the effects and reasons for ending a line in a particular place
- the resulting visual form of the poem
- the features of the sound patterns of the poem, particularly the repeated rhythms and rhyme.

Once these are recognized, it is possible to build up children's understanding of what the LINC diagram (Figure 6.1) calls the *sense*, including the use of imagery, metaphor, simile and ambiguity, as well as further aspects of structure such as diction and the poet's use of words, and also the way these words are deployed and placed in the poem, namely the syntax. Sense and syntax are fundamental as with all writing but they are not the starting points with the youngest children in primary school. A developing understanding of these aspects will be gradually built through the collaborative reading and writing of many poems.

Underlying principles for teaching poetry

Where, then, does this leave us in formulating the underlying principles for teaching about poetry in early years classrooms? Firstly, poems must be shown and read in order to demonstrate both the pleasures of reading poetry and what a poem looks like on the page. Poems should be chosen that are highly constructed, in order to make their point clearly; they should amuse, dazzle with words, bemuse, describe, play with words, and be laid out in distinctly different ways from other forms of writing. In so doing, a shared understanding of what counts as a poem is negotiated with children.

Secondly, poems must be jointly crafted with children, and it is through this collaborative and creative activity that the appropriate poetic features are discussed and pondered over in such a way that important teaching messages are conveyed. In order to do this, ideas are established about rhythm and rhyme as well as overall structure and line syntax. The precise and exact vocabulary to be used will be deliberated upon. If poetry is 'the best words in the best order', for that particular context, then to select the most appropriate words, some will be considered and some will be rejected.

Inevitably, the early years teacher will be doing most of the formal intellectual work in selecting the poems to read and the forms of poetry to use for collective and individual composing. Crucially, however, pupils' knowledge of words will be built upon, as is the playfulness they exhibit when experimenting with rhythm, rhyme and song which are a central part of the playground culture that exists away from the eyes and ears of adult authority.

The third and final principle is that children will learn through *doing*, not by being given theoretical abstractions and then applying the theory to practice, but by learning and discussing real poems, rhymes and rhythms and then applying their insights to composing their own, in collaboration with others and as individuals.

These principles also need to underly practice when implementing the statutory requirements contained in The National Curriculum for English and clear objectives outlined in the *National Literacy Strategy Framework for Teaching* (DfEE, 1998), many of which are concerned with poetry.

Poetry in the National Curriculum and National Literacy Strategy

In the statutory Programmes of Study it is clear that in both Key Stages 1 and 2 children 'should be given opportunities to read and discuss a wide range of poetry and should write in response to a variety of texts including poetry. The reading materials read and discussed . . . should include . . . language with recognisable repetitive patterns, rhyme and rhythm.' In Key Stage 1, pupils 'should be taught to write in a range of forms, incorporating some of the differing characteristics of these forms. The range should include. . .poems.' Further, 'pupils should be helped to make choices about vocabulary and to organize imaginative writing in different ways, e.g. a cumulative pattern in a poem.'

Thus clear direction is given in the very areas described above in our underlying principles for teaching about poetry, although little illustrative detail is provided about what poems and which forms should be taught and when.

Conversely, the *National Literacy Strategy Framework for Teaching* (DfEE, 1998) is much more explicit and comprehensive about the types of poetry children should read and write, as well as when they should be taught to do so. In so doing, the document, now being systematically implemented in almost all primary schools in England, makes the differences between the structural forms of poetry and prose clear and accessible to teachers. What follows are excerpts from the teaching objectives that illustrate this:

In the *Reception Year* (4–5-year-olds) pupils 'should experience a variety of nursery and modern rhymes, chants, action verses and poetry with predictable structures and patterned language ... they will read and recite rhymes and experiment with similar rhyming patterns; and use the experience of poems as the basis for independent writing, e.g ... substitution, extension and through shared composition with adults.

In *Year 1, Term 1* (5–6-year-olds) they will 'recite ... rhymes with predictable and repeating patterns extemporizing on patterns orally by substituting words and phrases, extending patterns, and playing with rhyme', as well as using rhymes as models for their own writing.

In *Year 1, Term 2*: 'to substitute and extend patterns of reading through language play, e.g. by using some lines and introducing new words, extending rhyming or alliterative patterns, adding further rhyming words, lines.'

In *Year 1, Term 3*: 'to read a variety of poems on similar themes ... to use poems or parts of poems as models for own writing (e.g. by substituting words or elaborating on the text) ... to compose own poetic sentences, using repetitive patterns, carefully selected sentences and imagery.'

In *Year 2, Term 1*: 'to comment on aspects such as word combinations, sound patterns (such as rhymes, rhythm, alliterative patterns) and forms of presentation. To use simple poetic structures and to substitute own ideas, write new lines.'

In *Year 2, Term 2*: 'to identify and discuss patterns of rhyme, rhythm and other features of sound in different poems, to use structures from poems as a basis for writing, by extending or substituting elements, inventing own lines, verses; to make class collections, illustrate with captions; to write own poems from initial jottings and words.'

In *Year 2, Term 3*: 'to discuss meanings of words and phrases that create humour, and sound effects in poetry, e.g. nonsense poems, tongue twisters, and to classify poems into simple types; to make class anthologies. To use humorous verse as a structure for children to write their own by adaptation, mimicry or substitution; to invent own riddles, language puzzles, jokes, nonsense sentences, etc., derived from reading; write tongue twisters or alliterative sentences; select words with care, re-reading and listening to their effect.'

The NLS *Framework* continues to outline extensive requirements for teaching about poetry as it moves through Key Stage 2. Quoted above are less than half of the teaching objectives that refer to reading, discussing and writing poetry in early years classrooms in the NLS *Framework*. The subject knowledge which teachers will need to understand and put into practice is considerable in order to comply with this initiative. This is not the place for a critique of the NLS *Framework*, but we believe that the issues of time have not been well considered. The time it will take to cover the teaching of poetry as well as the rest of the *Framework* in the allocated period seems over-ambitious. The implications for in-service training to develop teachers' knowledge and understanding purely on this aspect seems also to have been underestimated. There is very little devoted to the specific teaching of poetry in the INSET packs which are the main vehicle in the National Literacy Strategy for developing the understanding and skills of teachers in the teaching of literacy.

However, what does seem to be clear from the NLS teaching objectives is that:

- Pupils need to start with an awareness of rhyme in the context of rhymes that they know and recite and use these to generate further rhymes.
- Pupils will use the patterns in poems they read as the basis for their own writing. The structures will be provided for them to work within, which they can then extemporize on using a substitution of words and lines, for example.
- Pupils will memorize poems for recitation.
- As pupils become more familiar with poetry they will be able to identify and discuss the distinctive features such as rhythm, rhyme, alliteration and presentation/layout.

All of these will be incorporated into the principles for teaching poetry and form the basis for the various strategies suggested next, with a clearer emphasis on the essential features of poetry writing in our view.

Teaching strategies

The next section of this chapter outlines the main strategies and approaches that can be used to teach children about poetry. These strategies are, broadly:

- reading, reciting and discussing poems
- shared writing of poetry
- the use of planning aids.

These teaching strategies tend to interact with and depend upon each other; in particular, the writing follows the reading and draws on the insights from discussion through shared reading to shape the writing.

Reading, reciting and discussing poems

When experienced readers share a poem with the inexperienced, they demonstrate how poetry is read, in the same way that, as we have discussed earlier, they do with stories. The adult models the distinctive rhythms and patterns, emphasizing the tune of the poetic language.

Focus on meaning is best handled after the poem has been read and savoured, even perhaps after two readings. This may be through discussion of the subject or theme of the whole poem and in a way that relates the content to the young child's own experience. Similarly, we can talk about the effect of the particular words which combine inextricably with the meaning and the manner in which the particular words have been carefully selected by the poet for their quality of sound in order to support the meaning or atmosphere of the poem.

Certainly, the reading of the text will have been introduced as being a poem or rhyme, and in the sharing of it the negotiation of what counts as a 'poem', as opposed to other kinds of spoken and written text, has begun simply by applying the terminology to a particular performance of language. Anticipation has been raised. By accentuating during the reading the rhythm and/or rhyme, children begin to associate particular linguistic features with the term 'poem'.

With a poem, we repeat and savour words or groups of words for the sensation that they give to the reader, listener or reciter. For example, 'The Highwayman' by Alfred Noyes can never be read without returning to the line 'The moon was a ghostly galleon tossed upon cloudy seas'. Each new group of pupils must be included in the pleasure received from the image this metaphor creates in the mind.

Young children constantly repeat rhymes and lines of poems purely because of the sensual joy of the sound that the words make together. They are attracted particularly to alliteration so that tongue twisters like:

> Betty Botter bought some butter,
> But the butter Betty bought was bitter
> So Betty Botter bought some better butter,
> Better than the bitter butter Betty bought before.

are laughed at, repeated, practised and recited with vigour without a thought being given to the meaning. However, much is being learnt about the special qualities of this type of text, the particular and pleasing repetition of the same sounds and rhythm.

Making a collection of poems and poetry anthologies

Accessibility is essential. Selecting and gathering poems that have been enjoyed and then displaying the poetry anthologies in reading areas is a crucial way to assist the pupils' developing understanding of the poetic form. Collecting together, for example, a number of anthologies (rather than rhyming stories) in a basket labelled poetry and referring to these as poetry books is an effective way of reinforcing the particularities of the genre. Such collections might be shared between classes of each year group, to be used as a resource whenever there is a specific focus on poetry, perhaps for a week or more. Reading aloud from enlarged versions and drawing attention to differences in layout is also essential if awareness of the poetic form is to be developed.

Reciting well-known rhymes

Because of their central role in early adult/child interaction and popularity in playground culture, children and adults know many rhymes and poems by heart. This type of verse is thus a fruitful area for investigation of rhyme, rhythm, alliteration and sound patterns in poetry in general.

When working with nursery and reception children, a good place to start is with well-known nursery rhymes. Initially, the children can simply chant them together until they are committed to memory. 'Humpty Dumpty', 'Wee Willie Winkie', 'Sing A Song of Sixpence', etc. can be chanted and sung with great enthusiasm and pleasure. The rhyme can be clapped to accentuate the rhythm and the children are invited to join in. This is the beginning of an explicit understanding of the repetition of stresses in a line which form the basis of the rhythm or metre.

Pupils in reception classes should be encouraged to listen for the words that rhyme. This is not only valuable for their appreciation of the poetic form, but facilitates phonological awareness which is crucial for reading development.

The following is a description of an approach to teaching poetry writing in a reception class, using 'Humpty Dumpty':

First, the children learn 'Humpty Dumpty' by heart and to do so, the rhyme is chanted every day until all the class are intimately familiar with it! All the children recite the rhyme together, ensuring that everyone participates. This activity is especially valuable for pupils for whom English is an additional language.

Appreciating the rhythm and rhyme

The rhyme is practised followed by clapping the rhythm several times. The children then might look at an enlarged copy of the nursery rhyme and count the number of lines in the poem. In 'Humpty Dumpty' there are four stressed 'beats' to each line. Each line is clapped, counting the number of 'claps' or 'beats' in each. The children's attention can be drawn to the fact that there are four 'beats' in each line. The repetition of the rhythm in other poems can be investigated also to reinforce the idea of repetition of the rhythm, which lies at the heart of the way poems sound.

Continued use of the enlarged written version of 'Humpty Dumpty', through reading it together, whilst pointing to words, helps reinforce rhythm, sound and word match. The following discussion would focus on listening for and hearing the rhyming words. Rhyming words would have already been talked about before and generated, e.g. *cat, fat, rat*. Eventually, the connection is made that *wall* and *fall* rhyme, as do *men* and *again*, aurally if not visually. Further discussion can occur, that there are repetitions (*Humpty Dumpty, all the*) as well as the fact that *Humpty* and *Dumpty* rhyme too.

This process can be repeated to great effect on other simple well-known rhymes, for example 'Jack and Jill went up the hill' where the rhythmic pattern of the lines is slightly more complex in the six lines (2 beats, 2 beats, 4 beats, 2 beats, 2 beats, 4 beats) and there is a clear repetition of rhyme. Children get intensely involved in the rhythmic and rhyming patterns and many will subsequently work them out on other rhymes they know well, gleefully sharing their new findings with the rest of the class.

All through this sequence of teaching, understanding of the principle of repetition is being established, and the fact that it is central to these kinds of rhyme. Drawing attention to the way rhyme is written down on the page develops understanding of how the line breaks and the layout are distinct from prose. Initial questions or comments about layout can start like this:

This doesn't look like a story does it? What's different? Do you notice anything about the lines?

Having a storybook nearby (e.g. a book of fairy stories), to prop next to the rhyme so the differences are clearly visible, can help focus attention and the discussion.

The beginnings of writing verse

The children then might compose some alternative versions of Humpty Dumpty. This involves the technique of substitution. Some of the words in the original rhyme are left out and new ones substituted to compose a variation. This supports pupils' ability to rhyme, think about meaning, and to play with the words of the poem.

As always, this process is first modelled by the adult, and begins with some collaborative attempts through 'shared writing'. A start might be with a version of Humpty Dumpty with key words and phrases left out (Figure 6.2). Some thinking has to take place about the end of the first line, wondering what other objects Humpty might sit on (for example, a *chair, bed, pin*). A restriction to one-syllable words at this point might be wise! Then see if the children can think

Figure 6.2. Substitution used as a beginning to writing poetry

of some rhyming words for the first words (for example, for *chair*, perhaps *hair, air, fair*). Couplets can be made using the first two lines combined with the rhyming pairs generated (e.g. Humpty Dumpty sat on a bed, Humpty Dumpty lost his head). Lastly, the children can try to make the couplet into a complete and alternative rhyme by changing the last line. This is usually the most complicated, because children have to think very carefully about meaning (for example, 'All the king's horses and all the king's men, couldn't get Humpty a new head again'). Large and/or smaller groups might compose more than one of these, until all the children have understood and contributed. The children can continue to compose further versions of Humpty Dumpty using this technique. Figure 6.2 shows Alice's attempt. It reads:

> Humpty Dumpty sat on a chair,
> Humpty Dumpty flew in the air,
> All the king's horses and all the king's men,
> Couldn't put Humpty Dumpty again.

Perhaps realizing that this does not work, Alice read the last line back as 'Couldn't put Humpty Dumpty back again' which is closer to the number of stresses in the original. Alice shows that she is learning about repetitiveness of rhythm (first two lines match) but young children find rhythm difficult to reproduce and the final line, in both its written and oral form, does not match the rhythm of the original. However, Alice is detemined that the last line should make sense in the context of the whole nursery rhyme, and this is why her attention has been on the manipulation of the rhythm.

'Humpty Dumpty' reworked like this is a highly popular oral and written activity, particularly when more aware pupils invent risqué or rude rhymes! These are generally slightly older children who enjoy this activity and the chance it gives them to deconstruct and subvert traditional rhymes (as well as the teacher's authority).

Shared writing

This teaching technique is now enshrined in the *National Literacy Strategy Framework for Teaching* (DfEE, 1998). 'Shared writing' is a powerful strategy for demonstrating what experienced writers of poems do when composing, and in this case constructing poems. *The Framework for Teaching*, as outlined earlier (see Chapter 3), conceptualizes texts as having three levels: whole text, sentence and word. This is a simple but clear way of thinking through the aspects which can be demonstrated to pupils when composing poems through shared writing. With poetry it might be more appropriate to use the terms 'whole text', *'line'* and 'word' level. 'Whole text' refers to the way that the text is shaped overall and will include the layout and the format on the page. It could also include number of syllables and/or words that have to be used (e.g. in haiku and cinquains). This consideration concerns the 'discourse' or whole structure of the poem as outlined in the LINC diagram (Figure 6.1). The 'discourse' would also include patterning of lines (e.g. limericks, Shakespearean sonnets) or the rhyme pattern. Line level will refer to where line breaks occur, the metre/pattern of syllables within the line, and syntax. Word level refers to 'diction' (i.e. vocabulary) and/or the particular rhyming words.

Writing poems about the weather

The following description is a sequence of work completed in a Year 1 class and is used to illustrate how the *whole text, sentence* and *word levels* can be taught through shared writing.

The context for the writing of the poem was a topic concerned with weather. Some time was spent reading and then writing some weather poems as a class. Some poems were read from an anthology helpfully entitled *Weather Poems* (OUP). The children were invited to concentrate on the poems, to listen to the words and the way that they describe the subject matter well and also to enjoy the repeating sounds the poets used. (As you might imagine, onomatopoeia and alliteration were common features in these poems!)

Having listened to several poems, a discussion might take place on the issue of choice of vocabulary which might follow this line of argument. In order to write poems a poet needs good tools and the tools of the poet's trade are words so there is a need to generate lists of words before starting to compose.

Teacher and children might discuss some of the word meanings, rhythms, repetition of words and sounds, as well as description. This and the next stage works well in smaller groups of approximately six children of mixed ability.

First, generate as many words as possible about weather and write all words brainstormed onto a large sheet of paper attached to an easel. Next, look to see if they can be combined into a poetic form, which would create an effect. This is crucially where the teacher, as the more experienced writer, is brought to the centre, by demonstrating how the words can be shaped and crafted.

Below are two examples of what then happened. With one group, two words of the brainstorm had been written next to each other which when noticed caused much laughter. They were 'hot snow'. It was suggested that these might be used as the first line and then other pairs of words were generated from the original brainstorm that seemed 'funny' and contradictory to common-sense notions of weather. This the group did very quickly, repeating the pattern over nine lines. A title was decided upon, the draft read through again, and two words replaced for being more appropriate (or inappropriate in this case). The group finally arrived at the following:

FUNNY WEATHER
Hot snow,
Sunny rain,
Cold summer,
Snowy rain,
Sweaty snowman,
Purple snowcake,
Blue sun,
Quiet thunder,
Snowdogs barking.

This was the most popular of the five poems composed by the class over the morning as it communicated its purpose clearly, namely, to amuse. The poem was written neatly into the ready-made blank big book and the children demanded many readings and re-readings.

This poem appealed to us too, as the juxtaposition of what initially seem to be contradictory words, creating some interesting (and odd) images, as well as throwing up descriptions of common occurrences (cold summers in particular). 'Quiet thunder' is an evocative (and not unknown) phrase, while 'snowdogs barking' is amusing as well as thought-provoking. Thus, through the suggested form of two seemingly contradictory words on each line, children's understandings of how poetry operates are supported. This occurs at the whole text level including how the poem has a common, repetitive internal form and is laid out on the page. Repetition of the structure of each line is constant through the poem and it is clear that the layout is significantly different from other forms of writing. This kind of discussion also facilitates their understanding at the sentence/line level. At the word level the careful use of a particular vocabulary, and the bringing together of those particular words in this specific way, also helps to develop the understanding of the use of imagery and the effect created through the use of, in this case, contradiction, technically an oxymoron.

The second poem from this class was not quite as effective but it still is a worthy attempt for young children. The words were generated in the same way. Then on inspecting the results of the brainstorm, many words were seen to be describing rainy weather so a focus on rain and its effects was suggested as the subject, the purpose being to describe rainy days. An idea was offered to start the class thinking: one child said, 'You get frogs in the garden', and so the poem began 'Frogs in the garden' as the first line. We then tried to repeat the syntactic structure (or 'pattern of words'). After some lines were generated, it was suggested that the last line could be different to create a change of pattern for effect, to act as an indication of closure and summary of what had been described in the previous lines. The children thought 'We're happy!' an excellent choice – it introduces an element of surprise into the poem as well as changing the grammatical structure of the lines. This then became the completed first draft of the poem. As most of the redrafting had been done orally (see previous chapter) this was also the final draft. Some additional descriptive vocabulary, particularly some adjectives, might have improved the final product, but as ever in classrooms, time was pressing. The final version was written into the class anthology of weather poems.

RAIN POEM
Frogs in the garden,
Puddles on the pavement,
Rainmacs to keep us dry,
Rainhats on our heads,
Wellington boots on our feet,
Umbrellas to keep our hair dry,
Thunder, lightning and rain all together,
We're happy!

Again, as in the previous example, a great deal is being demonstrated about the way that poems are structured at the text and sentence/line levels as well as a developing awareness at the word/vocabulary level. In this instance, the disruption of the syntactical repetition by changing the last line shows a strategy for composing a poem that is more interesting for the reader, because of the unpredictability. This line also adds to the poem by describing feelings as well as material reality.

This particular strategy – of repeating the syntactical structure of the poem as well as trying to keep as closely as possible to repeating the rhythm/number of syllables in each line based on the model of the first line – is a common and popular one, contained in many books for teachers. For example, in Corbett and Moses (1986) the following example is outlined. It is an idea that works with classes from reception upwards. D.R. has used it, with the approach of shared writing, with younger children. With older children, the process is demonstrated by the teacher, then followed by pupils working on an individual line or number of lines using the same structure. It begins with the title and the starting point:

> *I wish I were*
> a green scaly turtle swimming in the Indian Ocean,
> a huge African elephant stamping through the steaming jungle . . .

By continuing to follow the line structure, pupils need to focus on the careful selection of adjectives and verbs to achieve the most striking image. In relation to the weather poems above, this is perhaps where those children should progress next, in order to develop their use of descriptive vocabulary in a structured and meaningful way.

Using whole poems as models

The last section of this chapter is concerned with using whole or significant chunks of poems as structural models for children's own poems and therefore substituting more substantial amounts of text into the structures already present. The following example is taken from LINC *Broadsheets* (1992) and describes using another child's poem as a model for younger children (in this case from Year 1) to emulate.

Treasures In A Box

The teacher read a poem called 'Magic Box' to her pupils:

> MAGIC BOX
> I will put in my box
> the lick of a tiger
> the grunt of a pig
> the kick of a horse
>
> I will put in my box
> the kiss of a lion
> the shine from the moon
> the sound of a trickling stream
>
> I will put in my box
> the bite of a kitten
> the roll of an eyeball
> the howl of a wolf

I will put in my box
the breath of a jaguar
the taste of the salty sea
the cold feel of snow

I will put in my box
the taste of fresh blood
the smell of old crab
the scent of a shoe

My box is the opening to human's mouth
with secrets in the molar teeth
Under the tongue is a twenty pound note
secretly hidden so no one can see

(an 11-year-old child)

The children were asked to close their eyes and imagine their own magic box, a box in which they had noticed 'there were things you couldn't hold in your hand'. The teacher considered that 'a broad structure supported them in creating their own poem ... these show how children adapted the structure to suit their own ideas and how well they could handle abstract ideas.'

Here are two examples composed by a 6-year-old and an 8-year-old, after less than an hour's work, from demonstration to completed first draft:

THE BOX OF BEAUTY
I will put in my box
the freshness of the air
the song of the nightingale
the beauty of the butterfly

I will put in my box
the slime of a snail
the sound of the seashell
the sparkle of a star

my box is full now
it is magic

by
SARAH
6 years old

THE CHILDREN'S BOX
I will put in my box
The tune of a whale's love song
the magic of pictures
the loneliness of a seahorse

I will put in my box
the sound of an old seashell
the scent of lavender
the quietness of a river

I will put in my box
the kindness of animals
the first wave of an ocean
the happiness of love

I will keep my box stored away
somewhere in my head

by
TESS
8 years old

As before, the clear and repeated structure has been explicitly drawn attention to and then utilized to create a very effective poem. During the composing the children have had not only to recognize and internalize the structure, which most do very quickly, but also to develop their skills at creating 'sense' using imagery and metaphor in particular, as well as choosing the 'best words'. They also produce poems of which they are immensely proud.

Planning aids

The final example in this chapter again uses the model of a poem for children to work with, this time written by an adult. The poem is read and discussed in anticipation of its use by providing structure for composing their own poems. As the structure is more complex than that of the 'Magic Box' poem, the children use a planning aid to help focus their attention explicitly on the overall, as well as the line, syntax.

The sequence of activities is based on 'Alone in the Grange' by Gregory Harrison:

ALONE IN THE GRANGE
Strange,
Strange,
Is the little old man
Who lives in the Grange.
Old,
Old;
And they say that he keeps
A box full of gold.
Bowed,
Bowed,
Is his thin little back
That once was so proud.
Soft,
Soft,

Are his steps as he climbs
The stairs to the loft
Black,
Black,
Is the old shuttered house.
Does he sleep on a sack?

They say he does magic,
That he can cast spells,
That he prowls round the garden
Listening for bells;
That he watches for strangers,
Hates every soul,
And peers with his dark eye
Through the keyhole.

I wonder, I wonder,
As I lie in my bed,
Whether he sleeps with his hat on his head?
Is he really magician
With altar of stone,
Or a lonely old gentleman
Left on his own?

(Gregory Harrison)

The activities will be outlined in detail, moving from the initial shared reading through drama to individual writing of poems. This sequence is suitable for seven-year-old children (Year 2) upwards.

1. Reading the poem

The reading of this poem should be preceded by a discussion about the number of ways that poems are shaped, including repetition of words and lines, line length, as well as rhyming and rhythmic patterns.

A first reading by the teacher of 'Alone in the Grange' follows this, with pupils following on an enlarged version so that they can see the text clearly. There is then a collective reading, perhaps followed by dividing the class into four to read each stanza in turn.

This reading is followed by a discussion of the meaning. This usually focuses on the following:

- The setting, i.e. what is the Grange?
- What is the poem describing?
- What does it mean to be alone?
- Do the children know any people who live alone that are talked about in this way?
- Do we really know what people who live alone are like?

Discussion follows on the outline shape and patterning of the poem – the repetition of the single word lines in particular, and how that builds the mood or atmosphere of the poem. Other aspects of rhyme and rhythm can also be talked about here. Exploring these areas should begin as a whole-class activity and then pupils should be organized into smaller groups to discuss the poem in more detail, so enabling all pupils to contribute their ideas.

2. Exploring further through drama

The second phase of work around this poem is generally focused on deepening children's understanding of the poem through drama. Much of what follows is an adaptation of a lesson contained in *Exploring Poetry 5–8* (NATE, 1987).

This sequence begins with a re-reading of the poem and a reminder of what it says of the little old man. The teacher says that more can be learned about the old man and his home. A visit to the Grange is suggested and the pupils decide who they will be: reporters, curious neighbours, local children who have lost their football, and so on.

The conditions of the drama are then negotiated:

- Will they look through the windows or will their roles allow them inside?
- What will be the Grange in the classroom?
- Will the owner be at home?

The teacher 'in role' as the main character leads the children physically closer to the Grange. Pupils describe what they can hear and see
through the windows. The old man may be in. If he is, then there
could be an opportunity to ask him some questions. The old man (a
confident child, or the teacher, if the class have not utilized these techniques before) emerges and the pupils ask questions. They may need
to have some time out of role at this point in order to plan appropriate questions based on their knowledge of the old man. The children then question the old man.

At the end of the session the class come out of role and are drawn
together. Discussion takes place about the events of the drama. What
have they found out about the old man that they had not known
before? A final reading of the poem can be followed by a consideration of the question posed at the end of 'Alone in the Grange', now
that they know much more.

3. Beginning to compose

The writing part of this sequence builds directly on the insights into
the subject matter of the poem developed during the previous activities. Children have been given firsthand experience through the vehicle of drama to gain insight and empathy. Pupils can then use their
understanding of the structure of the poem to construct and compose
a class poem, followed by individual poems, concerned with feeling
alone.

The process starts with a re-reading of the poem and a consideration of the structure of the first and second stanzas. This consists of
repeated single word lines followed by two longer lines. It is worth
pointing out that this repetition is there for a purpose: it builds atmosphere through the emphasis placed on those words. The children are
then told that they are going to use the same structure to write their
own poem. They might describe the feeling of loneliness, and decide
which aspects they will choose to emphasize through imitating the
techniques the poet has used. A brainstorm, once again, is a useful
way to begin, thinking of words and phrases which describe feelings
and situations where they have felt alone. These will be their raw
materials and starting words for when they compose.

When a substantial word bank has been generated and written up,
the pupils are introduced to the planning frame (Figure 6.3). The
frame follows the structure of the original poem and is designed to
support them while they are composing. Composition begins through
shared writing, and a first draft of a poem using an enlarged version

Alone: Composing Your Poem

Imagine you are alone. Use the words/phrases and sentences brainstormed as a class, to write a poem using a similar structure to 'Alone in the Grange'.

_____   Start with 2 repeated
                           words that describe how
_____   you feel.

_____   Write two lines which
                           describe where you are.
_____

_____   Two more repeated
                           words that describe
_____   where you are.

_____   Two lines about what
                           you wish would happen.
_____

_____   Two more repeated
                           words.
_____

_____   Two lines to finish the
                           poem.
_____

You may extend this pattern if you have more you want to write.

Figure 6.3.   Planning frame for composing a poem

of the planning frame can be accomplished. During the shared writing, the brainstormed words and phrases on the board are used as a starting point for thinking, and not as a constraint. Questions are asked during the shared writing such as:

- What would be the best word to begin our poem, that would describe the atmosphere, what we wanted our readers to feel right at the start? What would we be feeling?
- Where would we be when we were feeling like that?
- How can we write that into the next two lines of the poem?

After composing one poem collaboratively, pupils are asked to compose their own poems using their own planning aids. While they are writing, the teacher's interventions are mainly concerned with vocabulary: 'What is appropriate and effective?', particularly which words are best used for repetition and whether alliteration might be an interesting device to use, as well as reminding children how to use the frame to support the structuring of the poem. Figure 6.4 is a simple example of what has been produced as a result of this process. Nichola was very proud of her effort even though there is the odd spelling and layout mistake. As with all the other examples used in this chapter, there is much evidence that the children are able to employ text and line structure in a way that enables them to make use of their own ideas and communicate them clearly. Nichola is using repetition to heighten the effect of her words on the reader. The most effective

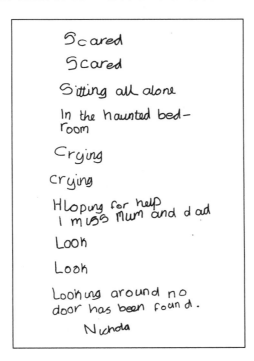

Figure 6.4. Nichola's 'Alone' poem

part of the poem is where the repetition of words and rhyme are combined in an evocative image at the end of her poem:

> Look
> Look
> Looking around no
> door has been found.

This is an appropriate example with which to finish this chapter. It demonstrates clearly that a pupil has learnt how to utilize the key elements that are described by the LINC model (Figure 6.1). The 'sight' – in this case the layout and shape on the page, the 'sound' – the rhyme and other repetition of sounds, the 'structure' – the combinations of words in the lines including the choice of those words, and finally the 'sense' – using the imagery of a room with no doors as a metaphor.

Conclusion

In conclusion, we would want to reiterate that as children become more familiar with a range of different poetic text forms and syntactic structures, and if they are given more opportunities to choose and develop their own poetry based on the principles outlined in this chapter, their sense of and enjoyment of poetry will increase in power and sophistication.

In this chapter we have suggested that poetry is characterized by its:

- sight – appearance on the page
- structure – organization including repeated patternings
- sound – frequently rhythm and word sounds
- sense.

Children can be taught about poetic structure explicitly through the context of:

- discussing poems read
- reciting well-known rhymes and focusing attention on structural features
- analysing and writing variations of poems
- composing written poems with a more experienced writer
- composing poems on their own using planning aids
- composing poems drawing from a repertoire of known forms.

7

Using a Range of Non-Fiction Genres in the Classroom

We require of them (pupils) a kind of thinking that does not come spontaneously to the human mind. The urge towards it is there, but the possibility of its mature development depends on a long cultural heritage; and of this heritage the special literate ways of handling language form an essential part.

(Donaldson, 1993:54–5)

Language skills do not simply mature in the fullness of time; their development requires conscious cultivation.

(SSG, 1987:4)

Introduction

Literacy encompasses the twin processes of reading and writing, they are complementary and mutually reinforcing: the development of one provides insight into other (Chapters 1, 2 and 3). If pupils are to produce the type of writing that school and society demand, they need experience of reading and using a range of fiction and non-fiction texts and having their attention drawn to the distinctive structural and linguistic features of each. Young learners also need to understand clearly the purpose, audience and context for which specific texts have been written.

The *National Literacy Strategy Framework for Teaching* (DfEE, 1998) explicitly makes these links between reading and writing:

Teachers should use texts to provide ideas and structures for writing and, in collaboration with the class, compose texts, teaching how they are planned and how ideas are sequenced and clarified and stretched.

(DfEE, 1998:11)

Children need access to examples of these texts so that they can begin to incorporate the structural features of text organization, language, register and specific vocabulary when writing their own. This is a very powerful connection: as Sealey suggests, 'reading is linked to the production of equivalent texts by the children themselves' (1996).

Understanding non-fiction texts

As we have previously stated, children come to school with extensive knowledge about different kinds of text, because of the variety of ways in which texts are used and produced in the context of the home environment. They are also likely to have noticed that there are certain features that distinguish the different kinds of text. Even preschoolers probably know that a picture book is different from a shopping list in that it is produced, used and kept or discarded in entirely different ways.

Littlefair (1993) argues that 'the most common expression of meaning which young children meet is that of narrative', and we know, anecdotally, that most children will have had this rich experience of story. She continues:

> Children listen to narrative in conversation, to stories that are read to them, and they watch and listen to narrative on television. This means that they will have extensive implicit knowledge of the linguistic features of narrative. (1993:126)

By implication, children entering school will have much less experience of non-fiction text types. Although, in our view, this is an area that needs further research, we suspect in fact that, although preschoolers are more likely to listen to stories, they have more experience of observing information being written, in the form of shopping lists, forms and greetings cards.

If we consider the kinds of written texts children may have experienced at home and the kinds of texts they eventually meet, read and utilize at school, there is a significant disparity. Although there are many different types of information text, they can broadly be classified in a small number of categories:

Narrative	Procedural	Expository	Reference	Lists
Biography, information stories, etc.	Instructions, such as recipes. Explanations of how to carry out experiments, etc.	Illustrated books on one topic, usually containing structural guides such as contents, indexes, glossaries.	Dictionaries, encyclopaedias, CD ROM, etc.	Shopping lists, telephone directories, etc.

As Littlefair says:

> perhaps the most important non-narrative text in school is expository ... it is this register of language which presents the greatest challenge to readers and which is ultimately of the greatest importance for their development as readers and competent language uses. (Littlefair, 1993:131)

When pupils read explanations and descriptions they have to understand a text which is arranged quite differently from narrative. The differences occur mainly in the following ways:

1. The *register* – the grammatical structure of the sentences and the vocabulary used. In narrative the language is often complex and descriptive, whilst in expository texts the language is often terse and concise with significant amounts of specialized technical vocabulary. In addition, the passive voice is used frequently and abstractions occur.
2. The *complexity* of the texts children have to recognize and use. In narrative the connectives are more linear and easier to understand, in that the context, rich with the flow of a story, carries the meaning. In expository texts the cohesive devices are less familiar to young children, including typically such conjunctions as *however, although, therefore, consequently*.
3. The *texts* are also *read* differently. Narratives are read from beginning to end. In expository texts the reader usually selects the parts they want or need to read (e.g. finding out which mammals live in New Zealand). Many of these expository texts can be read in any order.

Thus not only is the language of expository texts very unfamiliar and different from popular storybooks and the spoken language of many pupils, but the way children approach them is also fundamentally different. Added to this, they are the text type that in the early years of school is read far less often, so that there is an imbalance of experience. These written forms differ and vary according to the purpose and function of the text, as discussed in Chapter 2. Readers expect texts to be written in certain ways based on their implicit knowledge of how these texts are used and constructed.

The importance of being able to read and write non-fiction texts

The text types which we wish to focus on in this chapter are recounts, reports and explanations which all tend to fall into the category of expository texts. It has been argued above that these are powerful text types with which children need to be familiar if they are to have equal access to the culture that surrounds them. This culture is the dominant one of school: 'the forms of writing selected are generally considered to be those often required in primary and secondary school settings' (First Steps: 16).

These forms of writing have developed in schools and academic institutions and therefore have to be taught to children in order that they can display their knowledge in these forms. It may be that these are not the most powerful forms of writing, but the forms that schools value more than others when pupils display their knowledge in writing, through essays and written examinations. Meek (1996) suggests that perhaps we need to challenge the accepted norms of the school rather than finding more efficient ways of teaching them. Particularly, she asks, do we know whether these increasingly codified and seemingly rigid forms of writing really are powerful in people's everyday lives or are they simply conventions taught to children to socialize them into the ways of school?

This point contrasts with Donaldson who argues that access to these text types is important if children are to have equal access to the culture that surrounds them. However, it is not simply access to these types of text which is needed but taking on the way of thinking that underpins them. Donaldson (1993) suggests that it is absolutely essential to introduce children to these 'impersonal texts' in order to help children think in particular ways. She says that the thinking is 'impersonal . . . not restricted to the thinkers' life experience'. Children need to learn gradually, over the years of school, how to participate in the impersonal modes of thinking and linguistic expression that are such an important part of our cultural heritage. Donaldson goes on to give examples of the kinds of phrases that represent this 'language of systematic thought', such as *one reason is . . ., what this means is . . .* People who cannot handle this type of language and the impersonal thinking it represents are at 'a gross disadvantage in every field of study from gardening to astronomy'. All people should have access to these modes of thought so that they can contribute and be critical, to take part in the most powerful discourses that shape our society. If they cannot they are excluded and relatively powerless.

Although Donaldson suggests that most 'well-planned help' will need to be in the later years of schooling, she argues that early years teachers are crucial for introducing children to these forms: 'the teacher of reading can start quite early to encourage reflective ways of considering the written word.' Thus the teaching we plan needs to incorporate non-fiction forms, as their absence will systematically disadvantage children by limiting opportunities for them to develop ways of thinking which are fundamental to participating in a wider, adult society. In this chapter, we will demonstrate that young children can be introduced to these forms, in meaningful contexts, and that they can begin to use them in their own writing and thinking, with appropriate adult modelling and support.

Helping children to become aware of the structural differences in order to produce non-fiction texts

Firstly, we have to have a range of non-fiction texts in the classroom both to read to, and discuss with children and allow them time to explore. As Meek says:

> The most important single lesson the children learn from texts is the nature and variety of written discourse, the different ways that language lets a writer tell, and the many different ways a reader reads. (1988:21)

And secondly, we write these kinds of texts collaboratively with children making explicit the structure and linguistic features of each, within the context of school activities.

The genres selected for discussion in this chapter are those that the genre theorists have argued are the most powerful text types as well as those explicitly required by the *National Literacy Strategy Framework for Teaching* (DfEE, 1998).

What is to be taught?

The Programmes of Study for English in Key Stage 1 (DFE, 1995) make it a requirement that:

> Pupils should be taught to organize and present their writing in different ways, helpful to the purpose, task and reader. They should be taught to write in a range of forms, incorporating some of the different characteristics of these forms. The range should include ... notes, e.g. lists, captions; records, e.g. observations; and messages, e.g. notices, invitations, instructions.
>
> Pupils should be helped to make choices about vocabulary and to organize ... factual writing in different ways, e.g. a list of ingredients in a cake.

Although it is a statutory requirement to teach children about the range of non-fiction writing (even before the *National Literacy Strategy* was implemented) there has been little guidance as to when or what the key teaching points should be for these literary forms. In the early years, the types of information text teachers are expected to teach are now as follows:

– In the Reception Year (4–5-year-olds) children are expected to experience 'simple non-fiction texts, including recounts'.
– Non-fiction writing is included in one teaching objective (out of 33): 'to use writing to communicate in a variety of different ways, e.g. recounting their own experiences, lists, signs, directions, menus, labels, greetings cards' (our summary).
– In Year 1 (5–6-year-olds) the requirements are more extensive. Children are expected to experience the text types covered in Reception. Attention is to be drawn to the layout and structural features of non-fiction texts (particularly expository texts: ones that have been deliberately constructed for schooled research purposes) including contents and indexes. For writing, pupils are to:

- produce captions for their own work
- make simple lists for planning, reminding
- write and draw simple instructions
- write labels for drawings and diagrams
- produce extended captions
- write simple questions
- use simple sentences to write simple non-chronological reports and to organize in lists, separate pages, charts
- write simple recounts linked to topics of interest, using the language of texts read as models

- write own questions prior to reading for information and to record answers, such as lists, a completed chart and extended captions for display.

- In Year 2 (6–7-year-olds) children should be introduced to, be taught about and produce the following types of non-fiction writing:

- simple instructions
- sequential instructions
- definitions and explanations of special interest words
- simple flow charts that explain a process
- non-fiction texts which include, e.g., use of headings, sub-headings, captions
- non-chronological reports.

Thus the main generic types that are expected to be taught are recounts, non-chronological reports, instructions, labels, captions and lists. The last we have discussed in Chapter 4. Here, we will concentrate on recounts and non-chronological reports as well as sequential instructions.

How do we help children to know about and produce these types of text? First we have to have a range of non-fiction texts in the classroom that we read to and discuss with children and allow them to explore. Second, we write these kinds of texts collaboratively with children making explicit the structure and linguistic features of each, within the context of school activities.

Structure and form

Recounts have been identified as the most common and familiar writing that young children are required to produce in school. The form is close to narrative being chronological and the anecdotal recounting of events in our lives. Pupils seem to have fewer problems with this form than expository texts, so it is logical that this should be the first to be taught.

Reports (or non-chronological reports as the National Literacy Strategy puts it) are not such a common feature of our everyday conversations, and the conventions for structuring them will not be an implicit part of most children's experience. This is precisely why having experience of reading examples of reports will be crucial in developing an understanding of form and purpose. This is more easily written than done! The kinds of texts that are usually found in early years settings, as part of the reading programme and the general book resources, consist mainly of narrative and recounts, with a substantial dose of poetry and rhyme included on a regular basis. Reports and procedural texts are less common (other than the odd recipe for cooking time). Schools and teachers will have to search for published versions of these texts, although the advent of the Literacy Hour has led to greater awareness of the need for report texts, to which publishers have responded. Another solution is for teachers to produce their own reports, recounts and instructions as a model for their pupils to draw on.

When do we write?

People write for a variety of reasons. We may write for a specific purpose, such as a reminder of what to buy in a supermarket. We may write in order to create a permanent record for others to read, enjoy, and/or follow. In school, we often write to display knowledge and to show that something has been learned.

The writing that children do mostly occurs at the end of any sequence of activities. Writing should be purposeful, and teaching the structure of the writing should never be the sole reason for children writing non-fiction. It is most meaningfully the end product. We use a *recount* when we are concerned with talking about recent personal experience, whether an event outside school or, more commonly, a collective class trip or visit. We use *reports* when involved with descriptions of such activities as science experiments or looking closely at cultural and natural phenomena such as plants and human physiology. We use *instructions* when we are creating some writing that someone else can follow to find out how to do something we have already done.

Children move from new experiences and/or observations, through discussion and reflection, to summarizing and organizing their thoughts in a written form for a particular audience. Each stage in the process is made explicit to children whilst encouraging them to keep in mind the reason for writing in the first place, namely the audience and purpose. For young children the most problematic part of the process tends to be the organization of the writing, particularly the typical structural form associated with these unfamiliar text types.

Writing frames

To help support pupils in the structuring of these forms, Wray and Lewis (1997) suggest the strategy of 'writing frames'. These 'consist of a skeleton outline to scaffold and prompt the children's non-fiction

> Although I already knew that
>
> I have recently learnt some new information about
>
> I have learnt that
>
> I have also discovered that
>
> I now know that
>
> However, the most interesting thing I learnt was

Figure 7.1. Example of a writing frame

writing, providing a template of ways to begin the text, connectives and sentence modifiers which give children a structure within which they can concentrate on communicating what they want to say, whilst scaffolding them in the use of a particular generic form' (1997:122). See Figure 7.1 for an example of a frame. Two of the following examples, report and instructions, use these frames as part of the teaching.

These explicit models for writing offer support at *text level, sentence level* and *word level*. The text already has its overall structure. The sentence starters model the grammatical register, which is typical, for the children to continue. The cohesive vocabulary of appropriate connectives is also present. Wray and Lewis are insistent that writing frames should not be simply given to children to complete. The model for teaching with writing frames is the same in principle as the model for teaching all forms of writing. The frame is most usefully introduced through discussion, with the teacher explaining the purpose, and combined with modelling how the frames are constructed and used. Connection made between the texts children have read and the writing they are about to compose establishes clear links. The teacher can then move to a collaborative construction through shared writing, using, adapting and modifying the frame as appropriate for the teaching purpose and the children's prior experience. Not until then are children given a frame to help shape and structure their own independent writing (and it may even be that some children will be able to use the structure without the need of the scaffolding of the frame, having internalized it from the discussion and demonstration). Once the frame has been used, the structure will soon become internalized and can be used as a mental aid.

Certainly there are advantages of writing frames. They:

- help maintain the cohesion of the whole text
- provide experience of appropriate connectives
- model the more formal 'register' of non-fiction genres
- introduce more complex vocabularies
- scaffold the appropriate generic form,
- prompt further thinking, e.g. 'a fourth thing we noticed was . . .'.

Frames enable children to achieve some success at writing and in doing so:

- improve self-esteem and motivation
- prevent children from being presented with a blank piece of paper – 'a daunting experience for some children who find starting a piece of writing difficult' (1997:123).

The dangers inherent in the use of writing frames are that the frames can be misinterpreted as representing fixed overall forms as well as the only way of phrasing parts of the text. In addition, the frames may end up as the reason for engaging with the information: the end product becomes a 'filled-in' writing frame rather than the occasion for organizing connected thought. Thus the frames have to be seen as tentative and malleable in their overall form and only a transition stage in the child's writing competence. They can easily be adapted and re-drafted by the teacher or pupils as and when necessary. In particular, the frame should not be used simply as a decontexualized exercise in learning discrete genres of non-fiction writing, but always within an overall purpose for communicating information or recording and reflecting upon knowledge.

Principles for teaching

To summarize the main points from the first part of this chapter:

- Children have greater experience of narrative texts and so require additional support with reading and discussing non-fiction texts in order to become familiar with the purpose and form
- Children need to use models from reading to inform their writing
- The generic forms of recount, report and instruction/procedure should be made explicit to pupils so that these forms are internalized and used in their own writing.

Teaching approaches

Raising the profile of information texts in the classroom

The first approach is straightforward: ensuring that a range of simple non-fiction books are read and the typical features and content are teased out. This includes all categories of story or fiction books as well as factual or non-fiction texts.

When reading non-fiction books aloud, teachers and other adults should explicitly discuss with children the content. This will include asking questions such as:

- What is this book about? (Looking at title, picture on cover, etc.)
- What can you see in this picture?
- Do you think this book is about real things or not?

These types of questions will lead to opportunities to discuss and categorize books according to purpose. Pupils can be invited to consider whether the book is an information or story book. Enlarged texts or 'big books' are particularly useful for this purpose. Year 1 and 2 children can also engage in practical sorting activities. For example, two hoops can be placed on the floor and a mixed pile of books can be sorted into story and non-fiction texts.

As children become more familiar with and have more experience of information texts, they will become aware of the structural features of the kind of information texts found in schools and so be able to use these in their own writing. This again is best done with an enlarged text so that all children in the class can see the book with ease. Attention should initially be drawn to the structural features for information retrieval, including:

- title
- the blurb
- contents
- index
- how the contents list and index relate to page numbers.

When reading a text from beginning to end, these organizational features are not so important. However, pupils need to know the questions or enquiries to have in mind as they use an information text. Retrieval devices help the pupil to navigate efficiently through an information book. Children can be taught to use these by having demonstrated the way that they can answer the questions we mentally ask of a text.

Exploring a range of texts

The type of non-fiction texts that children engage with in school tends to be expository texts. But children meet many more information texts in their everyday life. An effective way of acknowledging this is to make a collection of the different types of information texts that can be found. This will allow pupils to make explicit what they know of the use and purpose of information texts from which the teacher can build. Introducing a 'lucky dip' bag filled with a wide range of texts is an excellent way to manage this activity. In the bag will be an assortment of texts including diaries, recipe books, bus tickets, maps, photographs and photograph albums, newspapers, food packaging, magazines, instructions from electrical goods, carrier bags, cheque books, video boxes, TV listings, magazines, local trade telephone directories (e.g. *Thompsons*), and so on. The children will have a 'lucky dip', and discussion and fun follow.

As each text is drawn from the bag we ask:

- What is it?
- Where does it come from?
- Who uses it?
- What does it tell us?

Categorization of the texts follows.

Teaching different text forms

Each of the following sections contains an example how a particular form of writing can be taught to children. Each example is preceded by a brief outline of the purpose and the typical features of the text type.

Teaching recounts

When teaching recounts, it is necessary to have a clear idea of purpose, structure and linguistic features. The *purpose* of recounts is to re-tell events to entertain or inform. The *typical structure* is as follows:

- an orientation to set the scene
- events in sequential time order
- a closing statement (re-orientation) which is optional
- an evaluation, which is also optional.

The important *linguistic features* are:

- use of simple past tense
- presence of cohesive words to do with time, e.g. *later, after, then, before.*

The following are ways that this can be taught.

Example 1. Oral news

Young children are always very keen to tell their classmates about events in their lives. Teaching about what to include in an oral recount, principally through modelling, helps to develop understanding of the structure of recounts. The process has been described in Chapter 5 under the heading 'Re-telling an oral story'. The process should start with the teacher telling some news herself. Before, during and after the recounting of events the teacher needs to keep up a running commentary on what she is doing, making explicit the content, components and structure (page 73).

Once the recount has been completed, it is important to make explicit the structure so that pupils can utilize it in their own oral newstelling. One way to do this is to write three or four prompt words on the flipchart to remind them. These are usually:

Who?

When?

Where?

What happened?

Important vocabulary related to time can be introduced and talked about (e.g. *first, next, then, after, finally*). These words too can be written up as a visual reminder for the children.

This process might be repeated when recounting other events by the teacher and when children are telling their news to the class or to a partner.

Modelling through shared writing and with the use of pictures to structure and sequence a recount is also an effective strategy. The following example demonstrates this:

Example 2. Dinner time

Early in the Reception Year (4–5 year-olds) to focus on recounts of common events is a useful way of drawing school routines to the attention of the children as well as demonstrating the structure of a recount.

This sequence of activities is based around the routine of preparing for and then eating lunch in the school canteen, which is a new experience for the children who have only recently begun to attend school for the whole day. The teacher suggested that the class should make a book outlining what happened at dinner time, as a way of recording the process with the intention of reminding the children what they have to do. The teaching objectives are therefore academic and social.

Making the book

- The teacher took photographs of the children as they prepared for and ate their lunch.
- The photographs were used to re-tell the events of the first part of the lunch-time break.
- The photographs also provided the illustrations in order to decide on the written element.
- Care was needed to structure the recount correctly.
- It was important that the children remembered the events in the sequential time order.
- Problems of photographs of two events that happened concurrently were discussed (i.e. some children eating their packed lunches while the others lined up to collect their hot school dinners).
- Two areas were under discussion: chronological order of events and the events themselves, as prompted by the photographs.
- Once the order of events had been agreed, the next step was to compose captions for the pictures which outlined the events. These were composed collaboratively and examples written on the flipchart by the teacher using the technique of shared writing.
- The children then chose a photo to write about and composed their own captions. If their independent writing was not yet at the stage where it could communicate to a reader without the support of the writer, the teacher scribed a conventional version underneath the child's (Figure 7.2 for an example).

The final recount read:

DINNER TIME
We wash our hands first.
We line up and go to dinner.
We eat our packed lunch.

Figure 7.2.   We wash our hands first

We collect our hot dinner.
We eat dinner.
Mary gives out the water.
We wash our plates, lining up for our pudding.
We eat yoghurt.

This demonstrates clearly the structural and grammatical features of a recount. The title succinctly summarizes the text. There is a full description of the children's experience of dinner time, from washing their hands to eating dessert, in chronological order. There is an example of a temporal connective – *first*. It is written in the simple present tense. There are many action words: *go*, *eat*, *wash*, etc.

The children's writing was collected together as a book and read to the class as a reminder of what they had to do. So we could say that this is an instructional text masquerading as a recount!

Another follow-up activity was to disassemble the book (easy in a ring-bound form) and ask groups of children to put it back in the correct sequence. This was designed explicitly to reinforce the principle of text organization underpinning recounts: the events occur in time order.

Developing expertise

As children begin to produce more independently their own written recounts based on their own direct experience, newstelling provides the ideal classroom context. As their competence grows, more purposes can be incorporated. Later, pupils will use recounts to reconstruct past events in which they have not been involved, for example in history, and begin to identify the form in the context of reading examples of diaries, biographies, personal journals and letters. The control over text structure should become more pronounced and the needs of the reader taken into account.

Procedural/instructional texts:

As with recounts, when teaching about procedural texts we need to have a clear idea of purpose, structure and the linguistic features.

Instructions are a very common form and have a clear *purpose*: to describe how something is done through a series of sequenced steps so that the reader can follow them. The *typical structure* is as follows:

- a statement of what is to be achieved
- materials needed
- the method, usually sets out as a series of sequenced steps
- sometimes a diagram or illustration.

The most important *linguistic features* are:

- usually in present tense
- use of cohesive words to do with time, e.g. *next, after, then, now, first.*

The following teaching sequence developing an understanding of the form and function of a procedural text was completed by a Year 2 class (6–7-year-olds). It exemplifies the teaching approach of moving from reading to writing with structured support from the teacher, including the use of a writing frame. This is well summarized by Beard (1999):

There are three stages to this approach:

1. modelling – sharing information about the uses and features of the genre (format, grammar, etc.)
2. joint construction of a new text in the same genre by pupils and teacher
3. independent construction of a new text in the same genre by pupils, with drafting/editing consultation with peers and teacher and publication/evaluation.

Example: Recipes for the big bad wolf

The children in the Year 2 class had previously considered some instructional texts and looked at the importance of logical sequencing and the use of cohesive words to do with time. We then moved to the following teaching sequence devoted to reading and writing recipes.

The children first received a letter, quite unexpectedly, from the Big Bad Wolf. The letter stated that the wolf had lost all of his recipes for child soup and stew and wondered whether the children would like to send him some more. This caused high excitement and revulsion, so the children immediately decided that they would compose recipes that would put the wolf off eating children for ever!

At this point we needed to consider the format and grammatical features of a recipe in order to be able to write one. D.R. displayed an enlarged copy of a recipe for Caribbean Spinach Soup so that this could be done. We read through and identified the three main components – title, ingredients and method – and talked about the essential function of each. D.R. then drew attention to the grammatical features of the method, particularly the use of the imperative at the beginning of each instruction (e.g. *Add* the rest of the vegetables) and a list was made of these verbs on the flipchart so they could be used in the writing.

D.R. then showed a blank version of the recipe structure to be used (Figure 7.3 for a filled-in example). Brainstorming the ingredients and the quantity of each happened next. Examples were:

4 leeks
2 large boys
2 tins of potatoes, diced
10 spoons of petrol
13 red hot peppers
5 gallons of vegetable stock

These kinds of ingredients should not make the wolf too suspicious of our intentions, but would certainly be unpleasant enough to put him off when he finally ate the meal.

D.R. and the children then composed together, through shared writing, the method, explicitly including the imperative verb at the beginning of each instruction. On reading through the finished draft, one or two minor adjustments were made to make the instructions more precise, and then the title was decided: 'How To Make Boy and Pepper Stew'.

By this time the children were itching to write their own versions. They did this in pairs. When they had finished their first drafts, D.R.

talked about the need to read through and check against the following criteria:

- Does the method follow a sensible sequence?
- Are all the ingredients used?
- Will the Big Bad Wolf know exactly what to do?
- Have verbs been used at the beginning of each part of the method?

The children then read their work to each other and/or the teacher and made any changes deemed necessary. Final copies were made and the whole lot sent off to the wolf. After a few days the wolf replied saying that for some reason eating children didn't appeal any more, and he was never going to do it again.

Figure 7.3 shows Jessica's recipe for 'Yummy Boy Soup'. The components of a recipe are all present. The list of ingredients not only identifies quantity but also indicates how they need to be prepared before the method can be followed (e.g. 20 spiders squashed). The language register of the method is consistent with the imperative form used throughout. Jessica also included two examples of cohesive words to do with time, *then* and *finally*, which they had been using in a previous session.

Title: yummy boy Soup.

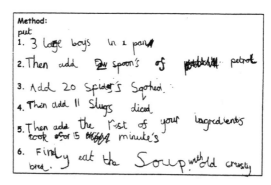

Figure 7.3.   Jessica's recipe for 'Yummy Boy Soup'

Thus the writing frame supports the composing at the text level, whilst the explicit attention to the grammatical features ensures that these are incorporated too.

Writing instructions for the preparation of simple food and drink can provide opportunities to carry them out practically afterwards to see if the method is clear and, if not, provide a powerful demonstration of the importance of redrafting. For example, the same Year 2 class had written some instructions for making orange squash (Figure 7.4). When they had finished their first draft, D.R. asked some pupils to read their instructions whilst he carried them out using some squash, water and a cup. It immediately became clear to the children that the instruction 'Put the squash into the cup' was not precise enough and had to be modified. Jack and Ashley's example (Figure 7.4) shows how they amended their writing in the light of this demonstration.

Non-chronological reports

The *purpose* of reports is to classify and describe the way things are. *The typical structure* of reports consists of:

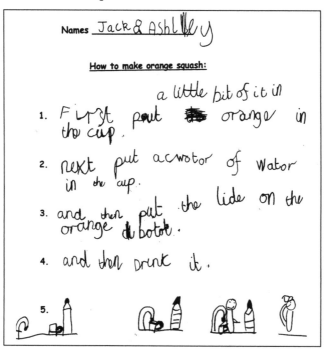

Figure 7.4.   Jack and Ashley's instructions for making orange squash

- an opening generalization/classification
- a description of the phenomenon, which will include some or all of the:
    - (i) qualities
    - (ii) parts and their functions
    - (iii) habits/behaviours or uses
- summary (optional)

The most important *linguistic features* are

- usually in present tense
- impersonal language
- contains subject-specific vocabulary.

Example: My favourite toy

The following sequence of teaching in a Year 1 class was part of a longer topic that had toys as its focus. To begin with all the children were asked to bring in a favourite toy to create a display for the classroom. Those children who did not wish to bring in a toy (or simply forgot) had the opportunity to look through a toy catalogue, choose a favourite toy, cut out the picture and mount it on card, in order that every child had an input into the class display and a starting point for their language work.

The children were asked to do a variety of spoken and written activities before the example described in detail here. There were information texts about toys available in the classroom, some of which were used for shared reading. The picture captions were discussed and used as a model for children's own captions for their toys on display. They formulated questions and prompts for the display so that visitors would be able to interact with it. Then it was decided that adults and children would need more information about the toys so that they would know what the toy was, what it was made of and how it could be played with.

This was the context for writing non–chronological reports about the toys. The reports would be collated into a book to be placed next to the toy display for children and adults to refer to. It was decided that we needed to describe what the toys were, what they were made of, how you played with the toy and why the owner of the toy liked to play with it.

As a result of this a writing frame was constructed (Figure 7.5) containing those sections. An enlarged copy was made for the shared writing part of the teaching sequence. The children's attention was drawn to the enlarged writing frame and it was explained that this frame would help them to write their reports about their toys. The frame was read through. A toy was chosen from the display and, together with the teacher as 'shaper' of the text and scribe, the collaboration began. Each section was considered in turn. It was made clear that the first section tells the reader about the piece of writing whilst the rest describes the toy and finally gives reasons why it is good to play with. The completed report was read through to check for sense, and sentence punctuation was also considered. The children then drafted their own non-chronological reports using the writing frame.

As the children were writing, smaller groups were supported intensively by an adult to clarify the task, to support and extend ideas, and help with some of the transcriptional aspects. Others were helped to do some simple redrafting. All children in the class completed an individual report about their toys. Once the writing had been completed, some children read their work aloud to the rest of the class and the structure and content were discussed as well as everyone's good work receiving praise. The writing was then stuck on a page in the class book of their favourite toys, next to a labelled sketch of their toy, which had been completed earlier. The book was placed by the display and read avidly by the children whenever they got an opportunity. The examples (Figures 7.5, 7.6 and 7.7) show that the teaching and the use of the writing frame enabled the children to write using

Figure 7.5. Courtney's report

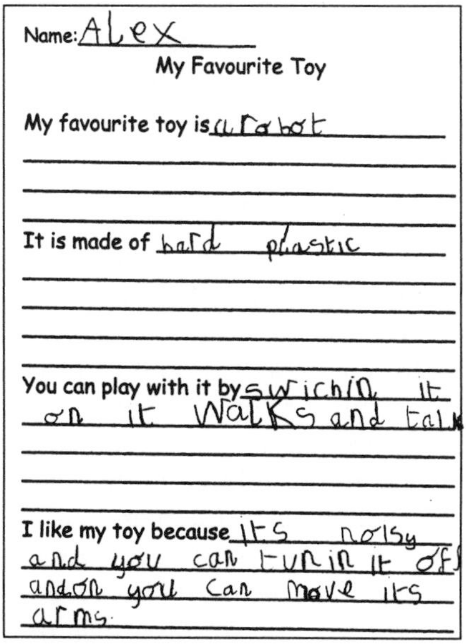

Figure 7.6. Alex's report

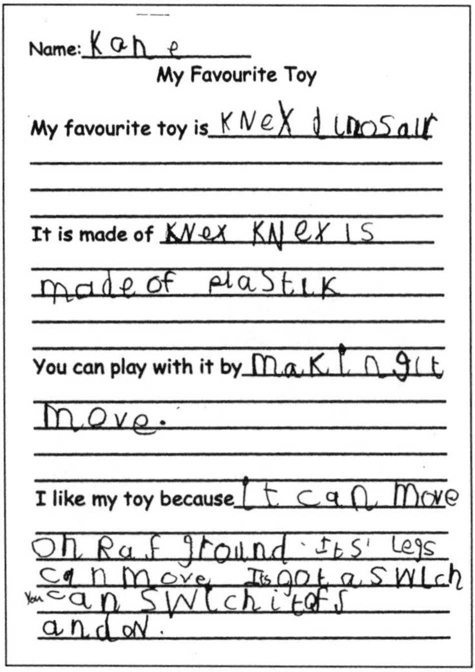
Name: Kane

My Favourite Toy

My favourite toy is KNeX dInoSaur

It is made of KNex KNeX IS made of plaStIK

You can play with it by makIng It move.

I like my toy because It can move on Raf ground. It's legs can move. It's got a SWItch. You can SWItch it of and on.

Figure 7.7. Kane's report

the conventions of the genre. The sentence starters ensured that the overall form was used and that the texts were cohesive. What comes over most powerfully is how these five- and six-year-olds (the work was completed in the middle of the spring term of Year 1) have used the more formal register consistently throughout, even though this was an implicit rather than explicit part of the teaching. For example, Kane writes:

> It is made of K'NEX. K'NEX is made of plastic.

Not only has the more formal language construction been used, but also he has clearly held in mind the reader, who may not know what K'NEX is.

In our view this kind of teaching is much the most useful context for explicitly or implicitly developing children's understanding of more formal language modes, in particular written Standard English. None of the children in this class used Standard English as their main spoken dialect and therefore are enabled to extend their language repertoire in a context that does not denigrate or undermine their own spoken language use. Because they are encouraged to rehearse orally before writing as well as reading their work aloud after writing, they begin to make the connection between *context, purpose* and *register*.

Conclusions

The above examples show that young children can write in a range of straightforward non-fiction forms given an appropriate context and focused teaching and support. Writing frames seem to be a very potent way of scaffolding children's learning at a crucial point in the writing process. The key question then becomes, when is the scaffold taken away? In the writing of both instructions and reports, this was the first time the children had been taught to write explicitly in these forms. In both cases, because of the needs of the curriculum, teachers moved on to different areas of language teaching. There was not enough time for these forms to be completely embedded in the children's minds through repetition and therefore when these types of writing are returned to most children will still need some kind of similar support. Wray and Lewis (1997) are at pains to point out that these frames are not a permanent support but must eventually wither away as children become adept at choosing the appropriate form and adapting the form to the task in hand. For the children whose work is included here, the time to remove this kind of support, particularly for the non-chronological report, has not yet arrived. Further progress would be seen by the ability to produce texts independently without the support of either adult or writing frame, after explicit introductory teaching. This is disclosed in more detail in Chapter 9.

Summary

In this chapter we have suggested that:

- In school children need to engage with a range of non-fiction texts.
- Children need to know the differences between fiction and non-fiction, including subject matter, language register, and the way they are read.
- The characteristics of a range of different non-fiction genres can be taught explicitly to young children.
- Writing frames are a very useful support when children are writing in particular forms for the first time.
- Children's writing should always be set in meaningful contexts that are familiar to the experience of young children.

8

Developing Control of the Argument/Persuasive Genre

Reading for information – book learning especially, as I practise it – is about thinking, wondering, and sometimes understanding, with the ever present possibility of being unsettled.

(Meek, 1996:12)

Introduction

Teachers and colleagues react in one of two ways when we suggest that children in infant classrooms should have the opportunity to engage with the generic form of argument and be taught its organization and structure. The first is one of surprise that anyone should want to teach about argument in the early years; surely the focus should be on narrative first. The second reaction is that the pupils are too young; they are not sufficiently intellectually mature. Implicit in both these reactions is that argument is seen as a 'superior' mode of discourse, on account of it involving abstract thought and a logical structure. It is considered that narrative is simpler and more likely to be part of young children's direct experience. It is, after all (and as we argued ourselves in Chapter 5), a 'primary act of mind', so perhaps it is appropriate to begin with story. The way that this book is structured might also give the impression that narrative precedes the writing of argument.

However, the position we take is that narrative, fundamental as it is, does not developmentally precede other forms of discourse and, moreover, there are valid reasons for including argument in our teaching in the very earliest years of education.

Argument as a 'primary act of mind'

Hardy contends that narrative is a 'primary act of mind' (1977). We would like to argue that argument is equally important in the thinking processes of young children. Children are able to use spoken language in order to argue very effectively! Argument is recognized by Halliday (1975) as one of the functions of language, since children learn language in order to:

- relate to other people
- gain a sense of mastery
- service their needs and desires.

The writing of argument is therefore as deserving of a place in the early years curriculum as narrative and other forms of chronological writing.

Wilkinson (1990) is also convinced that 'the other primary act of mind is . . . constituted of the variety of differentiating analytical activities – recording of evidence, evaluating, persuading, classifying, deducing, arguing and so on which we relate together under the heading of argument. Recorded developmentally, neither of these acts (narrative and argument) is primary.' But narrative has always been given priority in primary schools, as well as secondary through the teaching emphases of 'writing stories, learning to read mainly with stories' (1990:10).

Wilkinson's research into pre-school children revealed that the ability to narrate and to argue are present at a very early age. Wilkinson quotes two children (amongst others) to show how the conventions of an argument-based negotiation are displayed very early in children's development.

> Janet (3.6) is disputing possession of a doll with Cory (2.6). She offers her one in return:
> 'Cory, do you want this pretty one? Want this pretty one? Look, she has these flowers in her hat. Look, that one, O.K?'
> Janet supports her offer with two reasons – the doll has a hat and what is more she has flowers in it. This does not work so she goes on to offer a rabbit and when this is refused she tries a different strategy – if you are not sensible enough to accept this then it follows that you must do without:
> 'Oh, where's the bunny? Where's the bunny? OK if you won't have one, none!'
> Later the objects of contention are dolls' hairbrushes. For her right of possession of two hairbrushes, Janet appeals to an eternal law:

'Little babies aren't supposed to, but I am!'
But Cory, at 2.6, is not to be outdone, and can also appeal:
'I am posed (supposed to).'

Wilkinson (1990:15)

Both children quite clearly have the ability to argue points and are beginning to recognize that assertions have to be supported. As Wilkinson goes on to say 'the ... children use validations common in adult discourse – in terms of consequences, in terms of ownership, in terms of fairness, in terms of laws or absolutes' (1990:16). The children show equally impressive levels of implicit awareness of this genre, and of making a case, as we have seen earlier that they are capable of with narrative.

Wilkinson's work demonstrates that children have the ability to argue in these kinds of everyday, communicative contexts. Indeed, parents of young children will wonder whether any individual could possibly disagree. All his examples occur in spoken language and this is the place initially to start to develop the skills of argument. Children need opportunities for sustained oral exposition and interaction, guided and contextualized by the teacher, long before the translation into written language. These experiences embed an understanding of the purpose of this form of discourse, in addition to developing the ability to structure the language and so to hone its clarity and power to persuade.

Structuring argument

The definition of argument used in this chapter is narrower than Wilkinson's quoted above. Argument is defined here as being essentially persuasive, and is concerned with promoting a point of view. There are two aspects to promoting a particular viewpoint. Firstly, we need to have a view to argue: a subject that we feel strongly about, one where other people might disagree or hold differing positions from our own. Secondly, and related to the first point made, there has to be understanding that when we argue we need to acknowledge that there are two (or more) sides to our argument. Although we argue for one point of view, it is necessary to take into account and deal with the likely counter-arguments. (It is this that young children have difficulties with from both an intellectual and a developmental position, the ability to de-centre and stand outside of oneself and that viewpoint.) This recognition might be implicit with no direct reference to the other view, or counter-arguments can be explicitly mentioned in order to demonstrate their falsity.

Therefore, in order to construct an argument it is necessary to:

- have a genuine purpose and the motivation to argue
- have a clear understanding of the way to argue coherently
- be able to use the agreed conventions, both spoken and written, in order to be understood.

Purposes for argument

So that young children can come to terms with the complexity of constructing an argument, the role of the teacher is to provide a context within which children can argue a point of view. The skill is to find subjects close to children's own experience and concerns and with which they might wish to engage. With these clear purposes in mind, adults then have to demonstrate explicitly the conventional ways to structure such discourse in the context of the classroom. As primary teachers, we might believe that our young pupils' lack of experience of life renders them unable to argue about anything more significant than whose turn it is to play with a favourite toy. However, it is *our* responsibility to introduce pupils to the broader issues outside their immediate, everyday experience. It is through injecting controversy into the subject areas that children do know about, but had not appreciated involve differing points of view, that we can begin to construct a context for developing an argument. In so doing we can also provide a clear purpose and motivation for engaging in the research process.

Teachers might ask young children to consider questions which may introduce them to areas of which they had previously been unaware, perhaps concerning the concept of 'fairness'. For example:

- At playtime, should the boys always play football in the playground? (Or perhaps football shouldn't be played every day?)
- Should we eat meat?
- Why are animals kept in zoos? Should they be?

By both looking beyond children's 'common-sense' view of the world and asking critical questions about situations (and the result of the situations) of everyday life which are probably taken for granted (playground behaviour/activities, food, places we visit), we are able to introduce an element of 'disequilibrium', to use a term borrowed from Piaget. We can raise in children awareness of the results of human actions – and the need to question these actions and results – as well as a sense of cause and effect, of problem and solution and of moral responsibility. In order to motivate children, we believe that we must develop this state of mental disequilibrium in our work in school. Piaget contended that human beings seek to be in a state of cognitive 'equilibrium', and that learning only takes place when the equilibrium is disturbed and a person's current certainties are thrown off balance by new information or by the challenge of a difficult question. This 'disequilibrium' is an uncomfortable feeling that can be addressed only by discovering more in an effort to understand. Engaging children in discussion about issues which they had considered to be straightforward and uncontentious (particularly ethical issues) engenders disequilibrium. This motivates pupils to find out, to consider their new knowledge and understandings and so move back towards equilibrium, into a new state of mental stability produced by consideration, rejection, incorporation of ideas, or the adjustment of current thinking.

Mallett (1992) is forthright about ensuring that pupils have a clear motivation and purpose for the research process and insists that we do not need a great deal of information before engaging with argument.

> It is not the case that children need 'the facts' before they can cope with the controversies – the ethical element is part of the whole truth about a topic. The different viewpoints can usually be explained from the earliest stages in a way that children can understand. (1992:50)

As members of a society, children have to be able to appreciate that subjects often are controversial (in fact, almost every subject is!). In other words, a developmental task in growing up is to realize that there are many points of view, and that our own is only one, and may be no more justifiable than the others. This may derive from an event that has happened at school. Let's take the playground example: football games have been banned in the playground, some pupils decide this is unfair, whilst others may be relieved and support the decision. Another example might be an issue introduced as part of a topic (such as part of a topic on food) engaging with the health and ethical issues surrounding the eating of meat.

In the case study later in this chapter, an issue is introduced as part of a class topic based on 'living things', which provides the context for developing argument. Through creating a clear purpose for investigating an issue, reading and writing non-fiction texts can be placed to serve both children and teachers' purposes. Children can look at texts critically, both from the position of relevance to the current investigation, and also to consider whether the texts engage with the controversial nature of the issue or ignore it. As we have stated earlier, pupils need to be fully and actively involved in the learning process of which the research is part.

Writing should be purposeful, and teaching how to structure the writing should never be the sole reason for children writing non-fiction. It is most meaningfully the end product. These kind of activities develop children's thinking through discussion and reasoned argument, and thinking is a skill that requires deliberate fostering through authentic opportunities which enable it to develop.

Moving into writing: structure and form of argument

Wray and Lewis (1997) posit two slightly different generic types of non-fiction writing that include argument:

- persuasive text: which seeks to promote a particular point of view or argument
- discursive text, which seeks to present arguments and information from differing viewpoints before reaching a conclusion, based on this evidence.

As with several non-fiction genres, these two have a tendency to overlap and have many similar features, even though they can be seen as distinct. They are similar in that the author is still trying to persuade or prove to the reader that a particular point of view or a conclusion is the correct one. The difference is that in discursive text the differing viewpoints or pieces of evidence are likely to be more explicit than in a persuasive text. In discursive texts, the writer's position may not be stated clearly at the beginning, whilst in a persuasive text it is. The assumption underpinning a discursive text is usually that there is going to be an objective weighing up of the different positions, but of course, the author may be setting up aspects of the opposing argument in order simply to discredit them. Argument starts from a fixed position, discussion organizes the processes of arriving at a fixed position.

Wray and Lewis suggest that these two generic forms each have a particular structure (1997:119):

Argument	*Discussion*
• An opening statement (the thesis) often in the form of a position/preview	• A statement of the issue and a preview of the main arguments
• The arguments (often in the form of point and elaboration)	• Arguments for and supporting evidence
	• Arguments against and supporting evidence
• A summary and restatement of the opening position	• Recommendations given as summary and conclusion

Children seem to have particular difficulties with the kind of structures contained within these written genres. In particular, when we talk about argument, we need to acknowledge that there are two (or more) points of view or sides. Although the usual position is to argue from one perspective, we have to acknowledge and deal with the likely counter-arguments that we anticipate meeting.

Wilkinson (1990) describes a situation where seven-year-olds were asked to produce a written argument and they 'failed to notice that there were two aspects of the topic, and just argued for one'. It was only when a 'cognitive frame' was introduced by the teacher, which explicitly called for this dual focus, that the children began to adopt the 'for and against' type structure and began to see that some aspects of their experience might be problematic. The 'cognitive frame' is not in itself 'the issue', but it serves to shape the thinking. Thus through discussion with the children, a problem can be considered in terms of pros and cons and so the thinking organized. The question that Wilkinson gives as an example, 'Is playtime a good thing?', had to be considered in those terms, and by introducing the idea that playtime may not be a 'good thing' and then discussing and itemizing the positive and negative aspects, the structure of argumentative thinking is introduced.

So before approaching the formal structuring of the writing of persuasive texts and discursive texts, the underpinning principles, conventions and purposes for argument need rehearsing, with thought shaped through talk, and constructed by a more experienced user of language. It is the teacher who makes the whole process explicit to the children.

As already stated, consideration of the 'pros and cons' of an issue, the orchestrated persuasion of the audience, or the repositioning of our own point of view may be the end product in itself. However, there will be times when it is appropriate that the argument is written down and presented to the person whom it is the intention to influence.

Again young children, and older ones too, find the organization of this kind of writing problematic because it is likely that they lack experience of reading or writing this kind of text, in comparison with narrative, recount or instructions.

The place of the argument/persuasive genre in the National Curriculum for English

The Programmes of Study for Writing for English in Key Stage 1 (DFE, 1995) do not mention the argument genre explicitly as a form of writing to be taught or experienced.

In Key Stage 2 there is a requirement for pupils to be 'taught the characteristics of different forms of writing, e.g. argument, commentary, narrative, dialogue'. Furthermore, under Key Skills it states 'they should be encouraged to make judgements about when a particular tone, style, format or choice is appropriate'. The implication here is that narrative precedes argument (although this has never been justified in any government documentation), and that in Key Stage 2, argument is one of the possibilities that teachers can draw on, but there is no explicit guidance on what style, tone, format or vocabulary is appropriate to this form.

The place of the argument/persuasive genre in the National Literacy Strategy Framework for Teaching

There are clear and unequivocal objectives for reading and writing information texts from the Reception Year to Year 6. This is one of the undoubted strengths of the NLS *Framework*.

However, there is no mention of argument, defined as persuasive or discursive texts, at all, whether read or written, in relation to young children. These types of texts are only introduced in the NLS *Framework* at the end of Year 5 (10-year-olds), yet children have had experience of argument from a very early age, and perhaps more than they will have had of 'non-chronological reports' in their everyday lives. This leads us to question the model of cognitive development the non-fiction strand in the NLS is based upon. Nowhere in the NLS training materials or the *Framework for Teaching* itself is there any justification for this order of introducing pupils to the range of non-fiction texts. We believe that, if young children are limited to recounts, reports, explanation and procedural genres, then we risk neglecting the non-fiction text types that are most relevant to the children themselves.

Underlying principles for teaching

To summarize the main points from the first part of this chapter:

- Argument is an integral part of young children's experience and therefore should have a place in the early years classroom.
- Pupils need a clear purpose and motivation for engaging in argument.
- Pupils' oral ability to argue should be developed before and alongside introducing them to typical written forms.
- Persuasive writing has a particular structure which usually takes the form of an opening statement (the thesis), followed by the argu-

ments (for and against) and ending with a summary and restatement of the original position.

Developing spoken argument

The everyday 'hurly burly' of school life provides endless opportunities for teachers to help children develop their abilities to argue orally in more formal contexts. One example of how children's immediate concerns can be capitalized upon to foster this development is the judicious use of 'circle time'.

Circle time is usually used in early years settings to provide a forum to raise pupils' self-esteem, and as an integral part of the behaviour policy of many schools. All the pupils form a circle and discuss an issue or celebrate a positive aspect of behaviour. A common activity in circle time involves giving positive feedback to the 'star of the day'. Every child in turn is the star of the day. All children, in turn, say why they like the 'star' child. It is obvious how this activity promotes self-esteem, but it is also teaching the participants one of the key structures of argument: point and elaboration (even, perhaps, if the cons are not explored fully!).

Developing written argument

The case study that follows is a description of the process through which a teacher and pupils work, drawing on the teaching models of Mallett (1992) and Lewis and Wray (1997).

Mallett (1992:61) describes the stages of the process which are typically gone through when reading and writing non-fiction, in a school or academic context:

1. *Organizing prior experience.* This refers to sharing and reflecting on what is already known by an individual or by a group.

2. *Offering new experience.* This may mean a class visit, new information gained as a result of viewing a video or reading a text, consideration of an artefact, or an adult talking. This gives rise to:

3. *Formulating questions.* The new information combined with prior experience 'gives rise to a great number of questions, which can direct . . . book research'. This is the secondary experience.

4. *Discussion and planning.* Early discussion about new information found in books can clarify purposes and meanings. Then a 'flexi-

ble plan for future activity and the ways of representing their findings' can be agreed.

5. *Study skills and retrieval devices.* This involves finding the most
   appropriate books and then using retrieval devices (e.g. contents,
   index, page numbers) to find the relevant parts of the text. In addition, reading strategies are used, such as scanning and skimming
   to locate information wanted.

6. *Summarizing, reformulating and reflecting.* This stage includes oral
   summary, note taking, and reflecting on what has been found out,
   and also presenting the end result to an audience in written or spoken form, if appropriate.

This model is not seen as linear: stages are likely to overlap, occur in
a different order, and/or repeated in most cases. For example, it may
be the discovery of a new piece of information that makes us reflect
on our previous knowledge and thus raise questions that need to be
answered.

Wray and Lewis's (1997) EXIT model (Figure 8.1) has more steps
and is more explicit and detailed in the later stages. In our view both
are useful, as they complement each other, and a synthesis of the two
creates a more complete picture. In particular, Mallett's stage of 'offering new experience' needs to be incorporated into the EXIT model as
an explicit stage and not (we would assume) implicit in 'establishing
purposes'. If we are to motivate children to go through the research
process, then we must ensure that their curiosity is stimulated, by
exposing them to new information or ideas that cause them to want
to know more. Once this is done, the question, 'What do I need to
find out?' becomes an imperative and the desire to seek out that information and develop understanding is kindled.

Conversely, the latter stages of the EXIT model are more explicit
about the processes whereby we interact with text, record and evalu-
ate information found and then communicate it in different ways. The
authors of both models see them as not being linear but recursive.
Sometimes the process may not be completed at all. (After all, curiosity may be satisfied simply by reading and discussion without any
notes or final public communication being necessary. In fact, when
adults go through this process, this is overwhelmingly the case.)

These models describe a much more extended and complex process
than the one which children went through in the previous chapter to
produce writing in a variety of genres. In particular, as in the following case study, the process incorporates book research. The strategies which led to children writing recounts and instructions did not

EXIT: **Ex**tending **I**nteractions with **T**ext

Process stages	*Questions*
1. Activation of previous knowledge.	1. What do I already know about this subject?
2. Establishing purposes.	2. What do I need to find out and what will I do with the information?
3. Locating information.	3. Where and how will I get this information?
4. Adopting an appropriate strategy.	4. How should I use this source of information to get what I need?
5. Interacting with text.	5. What can I do to help me understand this better?
6. Monitoring understanding.	6. What can I do if there are parts I do not understand?
7. Making a record.	7. What should I make a note of from this information?
8. Evaluating information.	8. Which items of information should I believe and which should I keep an open mind about?
9. Assisting memory.	9. How can I help myself remember the important parts?
10. Communicating information.	10. How should I let other people know about this?

Figure 8.1. The EXIT model: stages and questions
Source: Wray and Lewis (1997)

require engagement with the research process by gathering information from textual sources and then using that information to reflect on knowledge and understanding.

A case study: on zoos

The Year 1 class lived in a mainly white working class suburb of east London. The children had been thinking about 'living things' as part of their topic work. The aim was to engage pupils in a task that involved developing argument, introducing them to an embryonic understanding of the written genre. We built carefully on the thinking of the whole class, shaping it step by step and allowing ideas to progress.

Activation of previous knowledge/organizing prior experience

The activity began with a discussion of zoos. Virtually all the children had visited a zoo, and the few who had not also seemed to be familiar with them. D.R. discussed the types of living things they had seen in a zoo. The idea of 'brainstorming' was introduced – noting down everything that the children knew about zoos in order to record the current state of collective knowledge in the class, and to provide the basis for finding out more. The recording of their ideas was achieved by drawing a circle on a large piece of paper pinned to an easel and writing 'zoo' inside it. At the end of lines radiating out from the circle each idea was noted down, either by writing or by drawing a simple picture.

The children were grouped into threes and asked to brainstorm what they knew. This they did enthusiastically. Figures 8.2 and 8.3 were typical of the class's recorded brainstorms. In Figure 8.2, the three children decided to use drawings of different animals in order to have a record of all the animals typically kept in zoos. They also noted the additional information that 'they are in cages' and 'people look at them'. In Figure 8.3 the children used writing only to record. They also knew that:

- animals are kept in cages
- there are strong smells associated with zoos
- zookeepers look after and feed the animals
- zoos are fun
- you can have a picnic on a visit.

The knowledge was shared by a whole class, each group feeding back in turn. D.R. collated the knowledge displayed on a large piece of paper (a very large one!). It quickly became apparent that there were three strands of information. This was pointed out and D.R. began to group the information displayed in the following way:

Figure 8.2. Aaron, Ryan and Sophie's zoo brainstorm

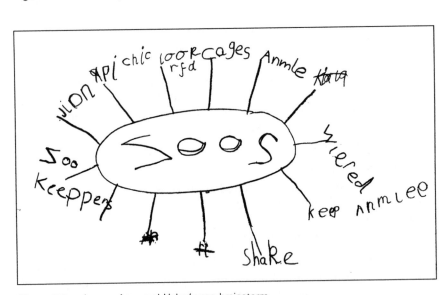

Figure 8.3. James, Amy and Haley's zoo brainstorm

- The different creatures to be found in zoos (shown as a list). This was by far the largest category of knowledge displayed.
- The experience of animals in the zoo (e.g. they are looked after by zookeepers, they get washed and fed).
- The experience of people visiting zoos (e.g. you have fun, you can see the animals).

No child at this point in the proceedings had offered any thoughts about the ethical questions that zoos might have associated with them. Once this knowledge was collated, we congratulated ourselves on how much we knew about zoos. Before the session ended it was explained that D.R. had just read a book, which was rather worrying and had made him think hard about animals in zoos. He offered to read it to them next time to see what they thought.

Offering new experience/establishing purposes

It was obvious from the first session that the children had never considered zoos as potentially controversial. They were an accepted part of their world. D.R. aimed to introduce some 'disequilibrium' to encourage the class to reflect more deeply on why zoos exist and in order to begin to explore the ethical dimension. To do this D.R. read the picture book *Zoo* by Anthony Browne (1992) to see whether this powerful depiction of the experience of 'the watching and the watched' would generate any concern, discussion and lead to research for more information.

The book was introduced by D.R. saying that he had always enjoyed visiting zoos and had not thought very much about it until Anthony Browne's story *Zoo* about a family going on a zoo visit. This had made him feel uncomfortable and wonder whether zoos were such good places for animals. The children were invited to listen carefully to the story and look at the pictures. After reading the book we discussed the issues which the book seemed to address:

- Why did the animals look so unhappy?
- Why did the mother in the family say 'poor thing' about the tiger continuously pacing up and down its cage?
- And then, at the end, why did the mother make the comment 'I don't think the zoo is for animals, I think it's for people'?

This led to some very puzzled expressions as well as animated discussion. The picture of one of the boys in a cage in his dream caused one or two pupils to comment that they would not like to live in a cage, as they would not be free. This led to a consideration of why the animals were in cages. It was suggested that this is so the people would not be attacked and eaten by the lions. They all then speculated that the cages were more to protect the people rather than being for the animals. The question 'Why do we keep animals in cages?' was asked and it was written up as something that might have to be investigated. As the discussion continued, D.R. began to point out that there was more than one point of view about keeping animals in zoos.

It was at this point that D.R. introduced a 'cognitive frame', a way of thinking about the two positions in the argument. To do this a large piece of paper was divided into two, on which was written 'good for animals' on one side and 'bad for animals' on the other. The children were intensely involved in thinking, as a whole class, about this issue. There were the beginnings of some very interesting whole-class discussion emerging, with some pupils directly replying to others, all listening intently when another child made a point and then helping D.R. as scribe to write down their initial thoughts. This is the final list:

Good for animals
- Animals get fed.
- Animals don't get hurt.
- Animals can't get out of their cages and hurt people.
- If people were locked in the cages it would be boring to look at.

Bad for animals
- Animals are locked in cages.
- Animals are taken away from their real homes.
- The babies might miss their mummies and get lost.

Whilst it might be the focus of further debate whether the third statement 'Animals can't get out of their cages and hurt people' *is* appropriately placed in the 'Good for animals' column, it was obvious that this Year 1 had made progress since viewing zoos as ethically unproblematic. In order to develop the argument and provide a clear platform for guiding subsequent research, D.R. asked the children to write down whether, following the discussion, they now considered that zoos were good or bad for animals. The group were also asked to think about which aspects they would like to know more about.

On the board D.R. wrote, 'I think zoos are ... because ... '. The examples reproduced in Figures 8.4, 8.5 and 8.6 are typical of the children's response. All of them demonstrate a clear understanding of the generic structure of persuasive writing, based on the discussion and the 'cognitive frame' filled in together. Amy (Figure 8.4) writes:

> I think zoos are good for people but I think zoos are horrible for animals I think zoos are fun to play in I think cages are bad for animals

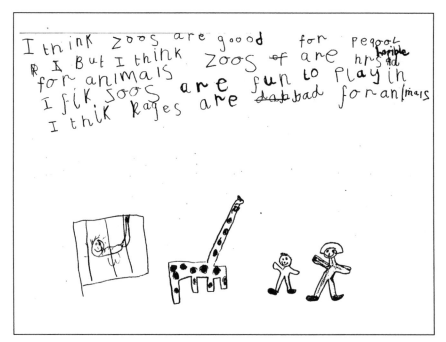

I think zoos are goood for peqool
R I But I think zoos of are hrs horible
for animals
I fik joos are fun to play in
I thik kages are dat bad for animals

Figure 8.4. Amy's view of zoos

'I tink its Bad For Aniemous Because
They Get tack up away From Ther
cRuctree.
and the Aniemos get loct up in a caGe i
tink its Bad.

Figure 8.5. Daisy's view of zoos

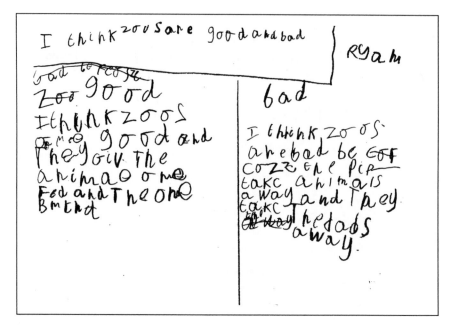

Figure 8.6. Ryan's view of zoos

Her two-fold thesis is clear and the points she wants to make to justify her position follow the same pattern. There is no restatement at the end but there is no real need to make one, as it would be very close to the original statement.

Daisy (Figure 8.5) wrote:

> I think its bad for animals because they get taken away from their country. And the animals get locked up in a cage so I think its bad.

This writing contains all the structural elements necessary. The thesis is stated: 'I think its bad for animals...'; there are two points made to support the thesis, then Daisy ends by restating her thesis and uses an appropriate conjunction to refer back, 'so'.

Ryan (Figure 8.6) was not so convinced by either position. Taking a classic liberal line, he decided there were strong points to be made to support both positions. He writes:

> I think zoos are good and bad

Good
I think zoos are good and they give the animals a home and are fed and they are bathed

Bad
I think zoos are bad because the people take animals away and they take their dads away

In Ryan's case, we have a clear use of the discussion generic structure. There is a statement of the issue followed by arguments for and against. What is missing is a recommendation at the end, owing to Ryan having not yet decided whether he would take one view or the other, or possibly he wanted to take the position that the two sides of the argument were equally strong.

These pieces of writing demonstrate that the children could construct a piece of written argument given the preceding discussion and teaching. The next step was to utilize their aroused curiosity about the nature and function of zoos to do some further research.

Establishing purposes/formulating questions

D.R. decided to continue to establish clear directions for further research by helping the children to formulate questions and to enable them to be more focused.

A new lesson began the day after the children had written in response to the themes of Anthony Browne's *Zoo*. D.R. reminded the class how they now realized that zoos might be more problematic than once had been believed. But more information was needed if we were to decide whether zoos were good or bad.

The question words *why, what, when, how, where* were written on the paper. The children were asked to think of as many questions as they could about zoos and the ones considered to be the most important would be made into a list. The questions that were eventually written down were as follows:

- What do animals do in zoos?
- What do zookeepers do?
- Are zoos good for animals?
- Are zoos bad for animals?
- Are animals happy in zoos?
- Are animals bored in zoos?
- Why aren't animals free?

These seemed to be the areas needing to be researched before a reasoned decision about the function of zoos could be made.

Discussion and planning/locating information

Where would this kind of information be found? Two sources were suggested: books about zoos and questioning a zookeeper at a zoo. The latter was not an option, as there were no plans to visit a zoo (with hindsight, to visit a zoo would have fulfilled many purposes –

the process to this point would have been an ideal precursor to a class trip). Books about zoos had to be the source. Between sessions (two-days) books were collected from the school library, the local public library, and from home and then used as the basis for our research.

Study skills/adopting an appropriate strategy

The selection contained a wide range of books about individual animals, very simple books about a visit to the zoo, as well as reference texts well above the reading ability of every single child in the class. The next stage was to select books from the collection and navigate through them in order to find relevant details that would help to clarify our thoughts. Teaching was needed on how to find out whether a particular book was going to give the information wanted.

The process the whole class went through was as follows:

- Reread and refresh memory of the questions.
- Read the title and then the blurb.
- Discard the books that were unlikely to be helpful.
- Look at the contents pages and demonstrate how they help to locate relevant information.
- Look at the index and read through the words to see if they promised any enlightenment.
- Go to the appropriate section in the book, read aloud, discuss 'Does this help answer any of our questions?'

Interacting with text/retrieval devices/making a record

Small groups worked together, each taking a turn to choose a book to search and find information. Most either used the contents list to locate a relevant part of the book, or chose to simply browse through using the pictures as a prompt for stopping and reading the text. This was a highly collaborative journey between the children and the teacher. Much of the reading was done by D.R., as many of the books were simply too difficult. There were other issues too. Firstly, most of the books written for young children were descriptive rather than evaluative. They were typically called 'A Day At The Zoo', and gave an uncritical view of the surface features of zoos. These books provided some further information about the zookeepers and zoo vets and their jobs. Although the questions that had been formulated were very general and related to ethical considerations, and they were not of the 'What food do elephants eat?' type, some useful factual information was found from some of the books. We also found out that some animals in zoos are there because there were none left in the wild. It was also discovered that some animals get very bored in zoos and their pacing around their cages/compounds indicates this. These points were noted.

A key issue was that only one book out of all the ones collected engaged with any of the ethical issues in which the class was interested, and that was the most 'advanced' and adult-oriented one. It was beyond the reach of this group of children to decode this book, but they were able to follow if the text was read to them. The relevant pages and passages were found and read aloud and the information was discussed. The technical language had to be explained, as well as guidance given through some of the dichotomies of the issue (e.g. animals removed from their natural habitat as opposed to preserving endangered species).

Reformulating and reflecting/communicating information

This further information, gleaned and gathered, enabled the children to construct a more detailed written argument, the result of which would be the basis of a presentation in a class assembly as other classes might be interested in our investigations and reflections. The writing frame (Figure 8.7) was introduced, using the teaching model outlined earlier in this chapter. The frame was constructed following closely the generic structure of argument and the guidance for constructing writing frames in Wray and Lewis.

We have included two completed frames (Figures 8.7 and 8.8). These are typical examples of the writing that the children produced. James and Martin's reads:

> We think that zoos are good.
> We have some reasons for this.
> Our first reason is because they get fed. Each animal has a different food prepared for it.
> Our second reason is they get looked after by the vet.
> Our last reason is the zookeeper cares for the animals.
> Although some people think that zoos are bad because the animals are taken away from their homes
> We think we have shown our point.

Lewis and Nancy posed an alternative view:

> We think that zoos are bad for the animals.
> We have some reasons for this.
> Our first reason is the animals get kept in little cages.

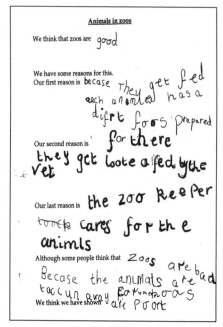

Figure 8.7. James and Martin's writing frame on zoos

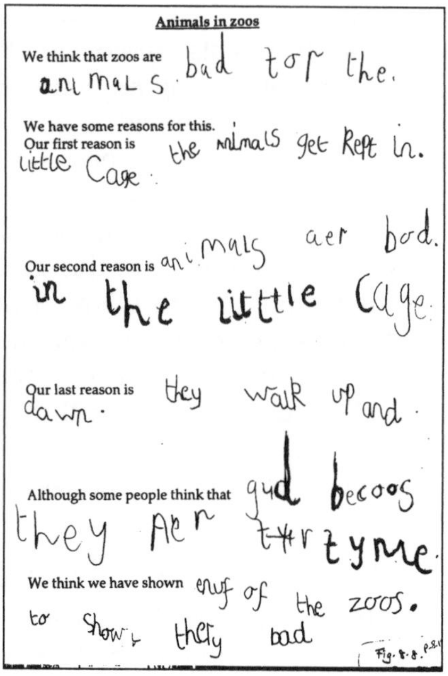

Figure 8.8. Lewis and Nancy's writing frame on zoos

Our second reason is the animals are bored in the little cages.
Our last reason is they walk up and down.
Although some people think that (they are) good because they are tame.
We think we have shown enough of the zoos to show they are bad.

There are a number of significant differences between these and the earlier arguments, written before the research and without the use of the writing frames. The children now include some of the information gained through the research process. They use this additional and secondary information to support their thinking. The care from a vet is seen as a benefit to animals in captivity, over those who have to fare without it in the wild. From the other side, the knowledge that the tigers' pacing up and down in their enclosures is a sign of acute boredom is so powerful that it dominates the whole of Lewis and Nancy's later thinking.

The use of the frames has scaffolded the children to present their arguments sequentially. In addition, the class have maintained in their own writing the more formal 'register' of non-fiction genres. The cohesion of the children's written texts is impressive. The arguments are focused and clear.

Our concerns about this work mainly arise from the use of the frame in the first place. Was it necessary? Would the children have been able to construct/develop the sophistication of their written arguments from the clear organization present in their earlier writing? Did the introduction of a single generic form constrain their ideas of what might be the best way of expressing themselves in order to persuade their intended readers?

The writing frame is useful when supporting children into the features of generic forms that they have little experience of, as we saw in Chapter 7 with non-chronological reports. This is not so necessary for argument where there seems to be a deeper implicit understanding of many of the underlying structures, developed through the kinds of spoken interaction embedded in the social contexts of their everyday lives that were exemplified at the beginning of this chapter.

So, for argument, the setting up of a cognitive frame, a much more skeletal scaffold introduced when the teacher discusses how the children might organize their ideas, is probably sufficient. The children can then use this as a prompt to construct their own argument and present it on paper, as Ryan (Figure 8.6) has begun to do.

Reflections and conclusions

When planning this sequence of work, it was hugely helped by the two models of the research process laid out by Mallett and Wray and Lewis. However, looking back over the attempt to implement the model, there are some further observations.

Considerably more time was spent with these young children on the earliest stages of the process outlined in the EXIT model than on the last seven steps combined. If schools and teachers are to use the EXIT model there needs to be clear guidance and resultant understanding of the relative importance and timings involved in the different stages. The problem with these models is that they are an attempt to clarify and codify in a linear way a process that is messier and more complicated when it occurs in the mind of the researcher. Stages are compressed or expanded, some stages may be redundant and therefore rarely occur. How often do adults write a written report after they have found a new piece of interesting information or heard an argument that transforms their previously strongly held views of the world? Stages will occur concurrently, and, crucially, some stages are more important than others depending on the motivation, purpose and linguistic experience of the seeker of further information.

Make haste slowly

It seems that there is a clear message not to hurry through the research process until the intellectual groundwork has been carried out thoroughly. The crucial beginning of the 'cognitive groundwork' is the offering of new ways of perceiving and interpreting old experience, which is not mentioned in the EXIT model. Thus, the fundamental reason for the need for any new information/understanding is obscured. Establishing purposes is much more than deciding *what* needs to be found out, as is suggested in Stage 2 of the EXIT model. *Why* do I want to find out is the crucially important question that needs answering before the rest of the research process makes any sense. As the EXIT model is the model used almost exclusively as the basis for the non-fiction strand in the *National Literacy Strategy Framework for Teaching*, this omission may have dire consequences. It could lead to the teaching of reading and writing of information texts as a decontextualized series of steps to go through, an empty exercise which uses specially constructed texts, rather than the learners being intimately involved with developing what they know.

The nature of research

The relationship between learners and the texts that surround them is one of a shared enterprise. This relationship has to be nurtured and capitalized upon by teachers. Children come to the texts because they want and need to make sense of the world they know. If a model is imposed that downgrades or ignores this basic curiosity and drive to interrogate what is around them, and neglects to challenge previously held beliefs, the learning will be reduced to an arid and uninteresting mechanical process.

This means that, in the early years, the contexts in which the research process is embedded have to be relevant, not based on long past historical epochs or geographical locations remote from the local area of the school. Readers come to the texts that teachers offer, with purposes in mind, both general and specific. The kinds of ethical issues used in this case study lead to more generalized enquiries rather than searching for specific pieces of information. This has consequences for the way the texts are navigated. The structural guides, such as indexes, to locate information may not be used, but the children want to read large parts of or even whole texts, and so accumulate further understandings to add to or to change previously held views. Adults usually read in this way biographies and other chronologically based information texts. If children are told to locate specific information only, they are given a false picture of the totality of adult reading of non-fiction texts.

This would seem to suggest that the EXIT model, with its implicit assumptions about looking for facts rather than extending areas of understanding, needs to be used critically and with caution. Drawing children's attention to the way that new information can change their views is an important part of this process.

The power of persuasive narrative

This leads on to another difficulty when considering the ways in which people read and write argument. Argument as a generic form does not have to be written in the formally structured way outlined above. In fact, most people will rarely experience persuasive text in this form. Often the most powerful arguments, the ones that really persuade the listener/reader, are narratives, the story of real people's lives either depicted through anecdotes ('Do you know what happened to me on the way home? Well I tripped over a cracked paving stone and nearly broke my leg. It's about time the council did something about it!'), spoken or written. If a newspaper journalist wants to make a point about the suffering of people in a war zone, or the untrustworthiness of politicians, we get a news story, not a structured argument.

Of crucial importance is the fact that many novels and plays have been explicitly written to put forward an argument (for example, *The Crucible* by Arthur Miller, written as a critique of the USA and its political system during the McCarthy era). Political systems have never underestimated the power of literature, and hence have not shrunk from suppression, censorship and persecution.

This effectively means that if we aim to teach children how to use the language of persuasion, we delude ourselves and them if we do not give the message to children that narrative texts can also argue and persuade and that this may be one of the main reasons for their existence. We must be clear that there are themes and purposes present in the narrative that seek to influence, but they usually reside between the lines. This must be a central concern of teachers, when collaboratively reading texts with children: to explore the multi-layered nature of the narrative (or poetic) text, and its ability to present points of view, whilst commenting critically on the way life is lived. Alongside this, when approaching non-fiction texts we need to be explicit about their highly constructed nature, exposing the gaps and omissions. In this way we can encourage critical reading, and readers who can read 'against the grain' of a text.

The six-year-old children in the zoo project learnt a significant lesson about being critical readers through coming to the books with ethical questions in mind. They soon found that the majority of the books treated zoos as unproblematic. The texts had left out a significant aspect of experience of animals in zoos and the issues that could be put forward by those opposed to keeping animals in zoos. The construction of a factual text is a highly selective task with much editing and decision-making about what to include and exclude. The result of this is to create texts which are at least as selective as fiction in terms of representing reality.

Anthony Browne's *Zoo* is the story of a visit by a family to a zoo and the bickering, conflict and tension within the family, as well as the depiction of bored and listless animals, is closer to the reality of many a young family's visits than the one depicted in the non-fiction 'A Visit To The Zoo' type books for young children.

This is one of the reasons why separating fact from opinion is so difficult. If someone's opinion means that they are economical with the evidence, does that mean the evidence they do choose to offer is counted as opinion? And which opinions underpin the presentation of a particular set of facts? That is the issue to be unravelled by the reader. Whatever it is, for these children to have realized that the books they collected did not tell the whole truth that they sought so avidly, means that they will be more circumspect when they approach the future reading of factual texts. At least they will wonder what has been left out as well as question that which has been included.

Summary

In this chapter we have suggested that:

- Argument is part of young children's linguistic and life experience and can be considered a 'primary act of mind' alongside narrative.
- Argument is typified by a clear structure:
  - an opening position/statement of the issue
  - the arguments and supporting evidence
  - summary and restatement/conclusion.
- The teaching of argument *is* appropriate in early years classrooms.
- Teaching about argument should be relevant to the experience and concerns of young children.
- The research process model utilized in the *National Literacy Strategy Framework for Teaching* needs to be the subject of further consideration.

9

Assessing Children's Growing Control of Genre

Children should be taught written language, not just the writing of letters.

(Vygotsky, 1978:119)

Introduction

This book has addressed the multifaceted nature of the writing process and its close relationship with reading, particularly in the early years of schooling. We have discussed how the sometimes competing demands that writing makes on the young child can be overwhelming. Conversely, we believe that young children are extraordinarily capable and that being able to operate within written language can both increase intellectual capacity (see Chapter 1 for the discussion of knowledge-transforming writing) and provide a mode of transmission of thoughts to others. Enabling pupils to become fluent in written language therefore necessitates a mode of teaching that concentrates on the interdependent but distinct aspects of writing, of which being able to represent the sounds of speech in print is one. Our main concern here, however, is teaching children how to structure their writing in a way that both takes into consideration the absent reader and adheres to the cultural conventions of discourse and form for different cultural purposes. Effective teaching and learning follow deep understanding of what the child knows and can do. This chapter, therefore, is a discussion of the ways in which teachers can assess children's overall progress in writing. We suggest that the assessment of their developing ability to express themselves clearly *and* with a growing awareness of the appropriate form for specific purposes can often be overlooked.

Providing opportunities to write for a purpose

Teaching with the learning objective of enabling children to have an increasing awareness of genre involves providing meaningful, *authentic* and challenging opportunities to write for different purposes. The school curriculum needs to offer rich opportunities for children to engage in thought-provoking discussion through which purposeful writing will follow. This writing will often be undertaken collaboratively in 'shared writing' or 'guided writing' sessions as suggested in the *National Literacy Strategy: Framework for Teaching*, in order to model and to support the attempts of embryonic writers. Throughout this book, we have given many examples of exactly this way of working with young pupils, offering instances of children engaging intellectually and emotionally with the content offered to them. Children identify wholeheartedly with problems posed to them through the vehicle of stories. See in Chapter 7 'Recipes for the Big Bad Wolf' for an example of how this was capitalized upon in a Year 1 class (Figure 7.3).

In this text, not only do the children demonstrate an awareness of the layout of a recipe, supported by the frame provided for their writing and the full discussion beforehand, but the language the children use is their own and echoes the discourse of cookery books: '11 slugs sliced', and 'Then add . . .'. The personal tastes of the authors come through, for instance, '3 *little* carrots' or maybe an empathy that wicked wolves, in common with six-year-old children, are not overfond of vegetables!

Assessment: what do children know and what can they do?

Sound teaching of quality only occurs when it is informed with knowledge of what children already know, and also, as Clay appropriately says, 'My position on good teaching is that it arises out of the understanding teachers have of their craft and never out of prescriptive programmes.' (Clay, 1998:130). The ability to support children in the compositional process of writing occurs through teachers knowing:

- the distinctive features of each genre
- what the child understands of those features through the close analysis of the writing produced
- how to make decisions on what the child needs to know next and what she needs to do to be able to use independently the features of the different genre

- how to provide meaningful and interesting experiences that make writing both necessary and purposeful, that is the creation of the context which will foster the intended development.

Transcriptional and compositional aspects of writing

Teachers do not usually separate out the different and distinct aspects of the writing process when they assess children's writing, nor perhaps is it advisable that they should do so. Assessment can become mechanistic in consequence. But teachers will need to focus their attention on a particular aspect of the child's writing for specific teaching purposes from time to time. What assessment schemes are there and which aspects of writing do they endeavour to assess? Educationalists in Australia and New Zealand (cited in Smith and Elley, 1998) do not separate the transcriptional aspects of writing from the compositional; they describe writing as being on a developmental continuum with stages referred to and with targets set. The Western Australian Education Department's Writing Developmental Continuum (Figure 9.1 at the end of the chapter, pp. 173–175) sets out the stages as follows:

1. Role play writing
2. Experimental writing
3. Early writing
4. Conventional writing
5. Proficient writing
6. Advanced writing

In Eggleton and Windsor (1995, cited in Smith and Elley, 1998), children's targets are classified into both process and product which the authors suggest fall within three levels of development: 'emergent', 'early' and 'fluent'. (Figure 9.2, p. 176) Whilst these three stages are very broad, and inevitably encompass a wide range of development, the process/product distinction is useful for us to adopt in this chapter. The step from 'early' to 'fluent' writing encompasses a huge amount of progression and we would break these two into more refined stages. However, what the Eggleton and Windsor scheme does offer is a separation of the features that are connected to the process aspects of writing – namely, the growing awareness of the alphabetic system (referred to as spelling in the early stage), understandings of conventions of print, punctuation – from the product aspects which involve planning and the organization of ideas in text, including a developing grasp of genre, and also reviewing and editing. These authors show how the two processes facilitate and augment the development of the other.

The levels of the New Zealand Curriculum which are referred to as *Written language: achievement objectives* make a distinction between the expressive, poetic and transactional categories of writing (Figure 9.3, pp. 177–178) in terms of the developmental challenges each presents to the pupil. This is an important issue. Children demonstrate variable mastery of the writing process, which is dependent upon the nature of the content and topic and their individual response to it. Together, the staff of a school might usefully consider the three schemes cited here in order to develop a school assessment framework for their own purposes. Having in their minds a pathway of the potential literacy development of their pupils is perhaps the most valuable aspect of the use of any assessment scheme which demonstrates progression clearly.

The developmental schemes outlined here are most useful in the day-to-day diagnostic, formative assessment of children's writing that is necessary in order to inform teaching, but not for the 'high-stakes' type of assessment (as it is described by Smith and Elley, 1998). By this they are referring to the National Curriculum Tasks and Tests in England and Wales. The intention of the English National Curriculum is that it was designed to enable formal, summative assessment of each of the prescribed levels of achievement of pupils. The extent to which this genuinely is possible is beyond the remit of this book to consider, but it needs to be acknowledged as part of the lives of all primary and secondary teachers (Figure.9.4, pp. 179–180).

Evaluation of a range of samples of writing

The type of writing assessment that we are suggesting needs to be embedded in whatever system the teacher finds useful, and it is based on the teacher having a broad and comprehensive picture of the child's developing control of writing, within which an awareness of genre and growing ability to compose texts will be encompassed. An understanding of the child's abilities to think through a piece of written text, and to structure it appropriately, certainly is not possible through the analysis of one piece of text as it might be thought we are implying here. The other point we need to make is that all analysis of children's writing needs an awareness of the full details of the context in which it arose and whether the finished result was aided or independent.

The following examples are assessed with the structural features of the different genres in mind, as discussed in Chapters 4–8. They draw also on the frameworks of development as described by Eggleton and Windsor (1995) and the New Zealand achievement objectives, albeit these lack sufficient detail on specific genres. Suggestions will be made for future teaching of the young authors of the texts discussed within a class setting, along with any learning experiences that might valuably be offered.

Monday 'news' by Alice (5 years and 2 months old)

Mummy is picking flowers in the meadow. She was happy. Daddy was making a cake inside. The End.

(Figure 9.5.) There is displayed here an awareness of the alphabetic code between the semi-phonetic and phonetic stages (Gentry, 1981) as discussed in Chapter 4. What is interesting for such a young child, is that Alice has a reasonably good grasp of letter/sound relationships (inside, makye/making), a small sight vocabulary (Mummy, Daddy, cake) and an embryonic understanding of punctuation but she has

Figure 9.5.   Monday 'news' by Alice

very immature letter formation, which we could argue, is one of the most straightforward aspects of writing to teach. Alice has written a recount but with features of the narrative fiction form. Her supply of the detail about how her mother felt makes this more story-like in the way she has handled the text, including the dramatic finality of 'The End' and a massive full stop. She describes her illustration, as children are often asked to draw that first, but we also have further information about Daddy on the edge of the picture almost out of sight, who is clearly adding to Mummy's happiness by making a cake! Alice is in Eggleton and Windsor's 'emergent' stage except for the fact that we do not know to what extent this child is able to talk about features of her own writing.

Eight months before (Figure 9.6) Alice's writing demonstrates that she was between the pre-communicative/semi-phonetic stage of spelling, e.g. no spaces at all are evident between words, although they are not very clear in her 'news' in Figure 9.5 either. Her understanding of the alphabetic nature of writing has progressed between the production of the two pieces of work – what about her ability to express her ideas? We would argue that there has been development, her ability to make her later recount more interesting and to consider her reader is shown. It is explained that it is Daddy who is inside the house and what he is doing. Precisely what teaching has occurred between the earlier piece and the later is not known. In the earlier piece, the teacher writes under Alice's lines in conventional script and expresses what the message of the text is declared to be. It is clear that Alice was left to copy it unmonitored, from the incorrect sequencing of the writing when copied. In addition, the handwriting is as immaturely formed when copying as when self-generated! There is no evidence of the influence of any formal handwriting teaching or support of organizational features of writing or the expression of ideas. In the main, Alice is maturing as she is exposed to stories and books read to her, and from which she is able to extrapolate some features of literary style.

Teaching suggestions

Alice now needs explicit support in writing narrative fiction. Rewriting stories following the reading of a well-known tale would be a good place to start. Discussion should cover the openings and endings of tales enjoyed, the implicit introduction of the notion of plot, and the agreed necessity for a problem in a story in order to make it interesting. Drama can be used as a vehicle for conveying this concept.

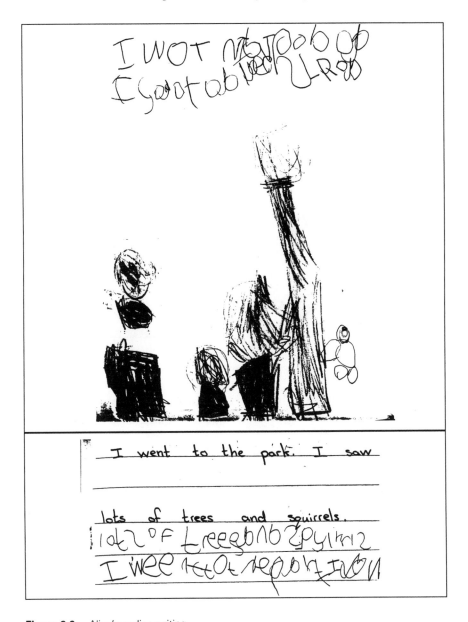

Figure 9.6. Alice's earlier writing

Capitalizing on the gathering of flowers in Alice's news, a drama taking place in a park might be acted out by the whole class. Children in role become park-keepers, people enjoying the park, people having a picnic, children playing, dogs being taken for walks, etc. The

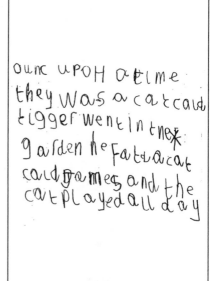

Figure 9.7.   Daniel's story

point that can be made is that the action needs to go somewhere. For narrative to become a story, it needs a problem and the attendant possibility of a resolution.

After a discussion between the children and teacher, it might be decided that the problem to be introduced is that someone is caught picking flowers. How the offence is handled, and what the outcome is going to be and so on, will need to be negotiated between adult and children, but the point is made well that now there exists a plot in the drama. The children will begin to have a conceptual understanding of the structure of narrative.

Daniel's story (6 years old)

Once upon a time there was a cat called Tigger who went in the garden he found a cat called James and the cat played all day.

(Figure 9.7). This child's work is in need of the same development as Alice's, more so, perhaps, as this is a recount more obviously masquerading as a story. Daniel has used the typical story opening and ending that he has heard many times, but the text fails to become a story as it is eventless. It needs problematizing. The same sequence of work suggested for the whole class in the earlier examples would be valuable here too.

Teacher intervention can be formal, such as basing a class lesson around what problems might happen in the park, or informal, simply suggesting as the child is writing, asking questions: 'I wonder what could happen? Do you think a cat might get stuck up a tree?' etc.

Colleen's poem (6 years old)

It started to rain one day I couldn't go out to play so I played with my toys without any noise and soon the rain went away.

Colleen shows a grasp of the essential features of poetic writing (see Figure 9.8). She has made a good attempt at making choices about the words she has used, the text has rhythm and she has employed rhyme, often a feature beyond very small children without banality setting in. What is missing is any attention to the poetic form. Simply encouraging her to make deliberate line breaks in different places from hers, which had been dictated by the paper width, would improve this piece greatly.

It started to rain one day,
I couldn't go out to play,

So I played with my toys,
Without any noise
And soon the rain went away.

Teaching suggestions

No poetry develops in a vacuum and this was no exception. A great deal of poetry reading had occurred in class, but showing children the shape and form of the poetry as it is being read is a very useful approach for developing the concept of a poem's shape. Discuss why the line-breaks are as they are and demonstrate on a sheet of A3 paper and an easel what happens if the line-breaks of the poem are altered. When children do attempt a rhyming poem (which should by no means always be the case), the obvious point to experienced, but not to novice, writers is that the rhyming words finish the line. This, then is a clue for children as to where the line-breaks should occur.

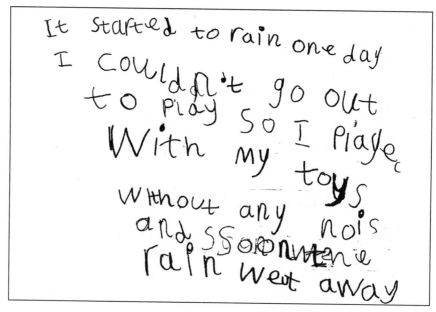

Figure 9.8. Colleen's poem

Procedural text

1. go out the park
2. and get the football
3. put the baby in the
4. goal and kick the ball in the
5. goal
6. winner one with most goals

The class were asked to write some instructions which would help younger children to play some games. This Year 1 child decided to write instructions for his baby brother (Figure 9.9) on how to play football. He has taken 'younger' to mean his baby brother, and interestingly considers that learning is best achieved by doing and that the baby will get an understanding of the game more quickly if involved and placed judiciously in goal! This boy has absorbed, and is able to use, the discourse of the procedural genre. The language is appropriate, he has employed the imperative voice and has written, with the dictatorial brevity of this genre, the instructions in a specific sequence of steps that need to be undertaken in that order. He knows how to organize the text: the format mirrors that of a science information text, instructing children how to do an experiment.

How to help this child to develop is straightforward in one sense in that a title would improve clarity immediately. In another sense the issue is one of conceptual understanding concerning the need for the writer to place himself in the shoes of the reader. This needs deeper thought and a series of sessions to achieve, as it is with the next level of performance that Michael will develop cognitively also.

Teaching suggestions

This child and others like him need to read again some instructions and to carry them out. During this process attention should be drawn to the importance of the title and the order of the numbering which shows the sequencing of an individual instruction, rather than the next line. Simpler games might be chosen for which the child writes the rules (e.g. hopscotch) and a frame used to help the children with the 'appropriate structure. Yumy boy soup' (Figure 7.3) is an example which can easily be adapted (and can also incorporate illustrations to aid the accuracy of sequencing). As suggested in Chapter 8, a very powerful way for children to discover whether their own procedural texts are genuinely useful for others is for classsmates to try to follow the instructions. This gives real insight into the needs of the intended user and leads to purposeful, considered redrafting by the author.

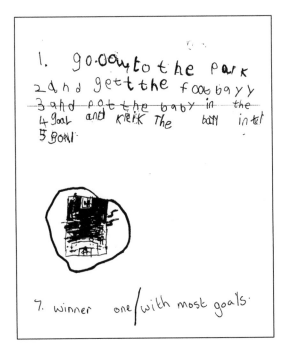

Figure 9.9. Michael's instructions for a game

Conclusion

In this chapter we have suggested that teachers need to analyse children's writing and reflect on which aspect of writing it is most important to focus in order to support pupils' progress. The complexity of writing understandably means that children cannot progress on all fronts simultaneously. The focus of teaching will alter over the passage of time in order that balanced development can occur. The compositional aspects of writing will be assessed for both the quality of the content and the appropriate organization of the text. These, we have argued, are inter-related and the development of one supports facility with which to handle the other. We have suggested some ways in which teachers can support young children in the way that they organize what they want to write and in this manner of working early years teachers will also develop their pupils' thinking.

Specimen Indicators from the Western Australian Developmental Scheme (adapted)

Phase 1: Role play writing
At this phase, children are experimenting with marks on paper, mixing together approximations of letters, numbers and other symbols. Five types (out of more than 30) of indicators of phase one are:

the writer–   assigns a message to his or her own symbols

– understands that drawing and writing are different
– places letters randomly on a page
– shows beginning awareness of directionality
– attempts to write his/her own name.

Phase 2: Experimental writing
At this phase, children realise that 'speech can be written down and that written messages remain constant'. Five typical indicators of phase 2 are:

the writer   – reads back own writing
– uses left to right and top to bottom orientation of print
– demonstrates one-to-one correspondence between written and spoken words
– relies heavily on the most obvious sounds of the word
– writes using simplified language structures.

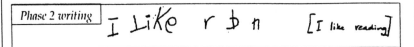

Phase 3: Early writing
At this phase, children write personally significant messages, and show some sense of sentence concept. Spelling is mostly phonetic. Typical indicators of phase 3 are:

the writer   – is beginning to use narrative structure
– experiments with words drawn from language experience activities

Figure 9.1. Western Australian Developmental Scheme

Phase 3 writing

My pet is a goat. She is wigle.
I feyd my pet ones a day. her
name is Sandey. She is very
friendle and soft. She is blak and
wigle and clean. She livse in a ben.

- rewrites known stories in sequence
- attempts to use some punctuation
- chooses letters on the basis of sound, without regard for conventional spelling patterns.

Phase 4: Conventional writing

At this phase, children are familiar with most aspects of the writing process, and are able to select forms to suit different purposes. Spelling is approximating the conventional (independent) phase.

The writer
- uses a variety of simple, compound and extended sentences
- punctuates simple sentences correctly
- demonstrates knowledge of differences between narrative and informational text when writing
- groups sentences into paragraphs
- uses adverbs and adjectives to enhance meaning
- uses a range of strategies for planning, revising and publishing own written texts.

Phase 4 writing

Dear Mr. and Mrs McKeown
Thank you for helping on all the trips but one. I
thought all those trips were fabulus. You were lucky
though you went on all the good ones. I learned
lots and lots on the trips. I loved being in your
group. I liked mapping the view at goat Island and
Mt Victoria. It was really tiring walking up Mt
Victoria, but when we got to the top it was work
it.
   You were wonderful on all the trips and I hope
you can come again.
        Yours sincerly.   Katie

Figure 9.1. cont.

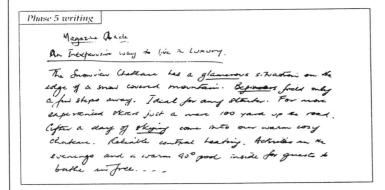

Phase 5: Proficient writing

At this phase, writers have developed a personal style of writing. They have control over spelling and punctuation. They choose from a wide vocabulary, and their writing is cohesive, coherent and satisfying. Typical indicated are:

the writer   – selects text forms to suit purpose and audience, demonstrating control over most essential elements
   – writes a topic sentence and includes relevant information to develop a cohesive paragraph
   – demonstrates accurate use of punctuation
   – chooses appropriate words to create atmosphere and mood
   – edits own writing during and after composing.

Phase 6: Advanced writing

At this phase, writers have effective control over the language and structural features of a large repertoire of text forms. Typical indicators are:

the writer   – develops ideas and information clearly, sustaining coherence throughout complex texts
   – uses abstract and technical terms appropriately in context
   – may choose to manipulate or abandon conventional text forms to achieve impact
   – takes responsibility for planning, revising and proofreading to ensure that writing achieves its purpose
   – reflects on, critically evaluates and critiques own writing and that of others.

Figure 9.1.   cont.

	Emergent level	Early level	Fluent level
Process-Focus	To have correct directional movement To leave spaces between words To use approximations according to the sounds heard at the beginnings of words To begin to use some high-frequency words	To use beginning and end sounds of words To use vowels To spell many high-frequency words correctly To use more correctly spelt words than approximations To begin using editing skills – to place fullstops – to place capitals – to locate approximations by underlining To begin to correct approximations by using word sources	To use editing skills – thinking about the message of writing – using most punctuation marks correctly – dividing written work into paragraphs – recording and presenting information in different ways – using a dictionary and thesaurus
Product-Focus	To be able to choose a topic to write on To use own experiences for writing To begin to talk about some features of own writing To be able to present a piece of writing for others to share	To understand that words carry many kinds of information To know that writing must make sense To be able to select from a wide range of topics and genre To be able to choose an appropriate title To begin to make some corrections to meaning To begin to realise that writing can involve a number of stages To begin to record and present information in different ways	To use variety in sentence beginnings To sequence ideas To use an increasingly wide vocabulary To write spontaneously to record personal experiences (expressive) To write descriptively on a variety of topics, shaping ideas and experimenting with language and form To write instructions and recount events in authentic contexts (transactional) To begin to explore choices made by writers and apply to own writing

Figure 9.2. Children's targets in early writing, classified by level and process/product (adapted from Eggleton and Windsor, 1995:13–17)

| Writing functions | | |
Expressive writing	**Poetic writing**	**Transactional writing**
Level 1 Students should: • write spontaneously to record personal experiences	Students should: • write on a variety of topics, beginning to shape ideas	Students should: • write instructions and recount events in authentic contexts
Level 2 • write regularly and spontaneously to record personal experiences and observations	• write on a variety of topics, shaping ideas in a number of genres, such as letters, poems, and narrative, and making choices in language and form	• write instructions and explanations, state facts and opinions, and recount events in a range of authentic contexts
Level 3 • write regularly and with ease to express personal responses to different experiences and to record observations and ideas	• write on a variety of topics, shaping, editing, and reworking texts in a range of genres, and using vocabulary and conventions, such as spelling and sentence structure, appropriate to the genre	• write instructions, explanations, and factual accounts, and express personal viewpoints, in a range of authentic contexts, sequencing ideas logically
Level 4 • write regularly and with ease to express personal responses to a range of experiences and texts, explore ideas, and record observations	• write on a variety of topics, shaping, editing, and reworking texts in a range of genres, expressing ideas and experiences imaginatively and using appropriate vocabulary and conventions, such as spelling and sentence structure	• write instructions, explanations, and factual accounts, and express and explain a point of view, in a range of authentic contexts, organising and linking ideas logically and making language choices appropriate to the audience
Level 5 • write regularly and confidently to respond to a range of experiences, ideas, observations, and text, developing a personal voice	• write on a variety of topics, shaping, editing, and reworking texts in a extended range of genres, selecting appropriate language features and using conventions of writing accurately and confidently	• write coherent, logical instructions, explanations, and factual accounts, and express and argue a point of view, linking main and supporting ideas, and structuring material in appropriate styles in a range of authentic contexts

Figure 9.3.   Levels of the New Zealand Curriculumn – Written language achievement objectives

Writing functions

	Expressive writing	Poetic writing	Transactional writing
Level 6	• write regularly, confidently, and fluently to reflect on a range of experiences, ideas, feelings, and texts, developing a personal voice	• write on a variety of topics, shaping, editing, and reworking texts to express experiences and ideas imaginatively in an extended range of genres, choosing appropriate language features and using conventions of writing accurately and with discrimination	• write clear, coherent instructions, explanations, and factual reports and express and justify a point of view persuasively, structuring material confidently, in appropriate styles for different audiences, in a range of authentic contexts
Level 7	• write regularly, confidently, and fluently to reflect on, interpret, and explore a wide range of experiences, ideas, feelings, and texts, developing a personal voice	• write on a variety of topics, shaping, editing, and reworking texts to investigate and explore ideas imaginatively in a wide range of genres, using the conventions of writing securely, and integrating techniques with purpose	• write clear, coherent explanations and reports, and debate a proposition or point of view, structuring well researched material effectively, in appropriate styles for different audiences, in a range of authentic contexts
Level 8	• use expressive writing regularly, fluently, and by choice, to reflect on, interpret, and explore a wide range of experiences, ideas, feelings, and texts, expressing complex thoughts in a personal voice.	• write on a variety of topics, in a wide range of genres, shaping, editing, and reworking texts and demonstrating depth of thought, imaginative awareness, and secure use of language, including accurate and discriminating use of the conventions of writing, and integrating techniques with purpose.	• write explanations and reports on complex issues, and debate in depth a proposition or point of view, structuring well researched material effectively, in appropriate styles for different audiences, in a range of authentic contexts.

Figure 9.3. Continued

Level 1

Pupils' writing communicates meaning through simple words and phrases. In their reading or their writing, pupils begin to show awareness of how full stops are used. Letters are usually clearly shaped and correctly orientated.

Level 2

Pupils' writing communicates meaning in both narrative and non-narrative forms, using appropriate and interesting vocabulary, and showing some awareness of the reader. Ideas are developed in a sequence of sentences, sometimes demarcated by capital letters and full stops. Simple, monosyllabic words are usually spelt correctly, and where there are inaccuracies the alternative is phonetically plausible. In handwriting, letters are accurately formed and consistent in size.

Level 3

Pupils' writing is often organised, imaginative and clear. The main features of different forms of writing are used appropriately, beginning to be adapted to different readers. Sequences of sentences extend ideas logically and words are chosen for variety and interest. The basic grammatical structure of sentences is usually correct. Spelling is usually accurate, including that of common, polysyllabic words. Punctuation to mark sentences – full stops, capital letters and question marks – is used accurately. Handwriting is joined and legible.

Level 4

Pupils' writing is a range of forms is lively and thoughtful. Ideas are often sustained and developed in interesting ways and organised appropriately for the purpose of the reader. Vocabulary choices are often adventurous and words are used for effect. Pupils are beginning to use grammatically complex sentences, extending meaning. Spelling, including that of polysyllabic words that conform to regular patterns, is generally accurate. Full stops, capital letters and question marks are used correctly, and pupils are beginning to use punctuation within the sentence. Handwriting style is fluent, joined and legible.

Level 5

Pupils' writing in varied and interesting, conveying meaning clearly in a range of forms for different readers, using a more formal style where appropriate. Vocabulary choices are imaginative and words are used precisely. Simple and complex sentences are organised into paragraphs. Words with complex regular patterns are usually spelt correctly. A range of punctuation, including commas, apostrophes and inverted commas, is usually used accurately. Handwriting is joined, clear and fluent and, where appropriate, is adapted to a range of tasks.

Level 6

Pupils' writing often engages and sustains the reader's interest, showing some adaptation of style and register to different forms, including using an impersonal style where appropriate. Pupils use a range of sentence structures and varied vocabulary to create effects. Spelling is generally accurate, including that of

Figure 9.4. Review of the National Curriculumn for English Attainment Target 3: Writing (DfEE, 1999)

irregular words. Handwriting is neat and legible. A range of punctuation is usually used correctly to clarify meaning, and ideas are organised into paragraphs.

Level 7
Pupils' writing is confident and shows appropriate choices of style in a range of forms. In narrative writing, characters and settings are developed and, in non-fiction, ideas are organised and coherent. Grammatical features and vocabulary are accurately and effectively used. Spelling is correct, including that of complex irregular words. Work is legible and attractively presented. Paragraphing and correct punctuation are used to make the sequence of events or ideas coherent and clear to the reader.

Level 8
Pupils' writing shows the selection of specific features or expressions to convey particular effects and to interest the reader. Narrative writing shows control of characters, events and settings, and shows variety in structure. Non-fiction writing is coherent and gives clear points of view. The use of vocabulary and grammar enables fine distinctions to be made or emphasis achieved. Writing shows a clear grasp of the use of punctuation and paragraphing.

Exceptional performance
Pupils' writing has shape and impact and shows control of a range of styles maintaining the interest of the reader throughout. Narratives use structure as well as vocabulary for a range of imaginative effects, and non-fiction is coherent, reasoned and persuasive. A variety of grammatical constructions and punctuation is used accurately and appropriately and with sensitivity. Paragraphs are well constructed and linked in order to clarify the organisation of the writing as a whole.

Figure 9.4.   cont.

References

A First Poetry Book (1979) Oxford: Oxford University Press.

Ahlberg, A. and Ahlberg, J. (1986) *The Jolly Postman*. Hong Kong: Heinemann.

Auden, W.H. (1963) *The Dyer's Hand*. London: Faber and Faber.

Baker, P. and Raban, A. (1991) Reading Before and After the Early Days of Schooling. *Reading*, April, pp. 6–13.

Balaam, J. and Merrick, B. (1987) *Exploring Poetry* 5-8. NATE.

Barton, M. (1988) *Zoos and Game Reserves*. Franklin Watts.

Beard, R. (ed.) (1993) *Teaching Literacy: Balancing Perspectives*. London: Hodder and Stoughton.

Beard, R. (1994) The writing process, in D. Wray and J. Medwell (eds.) *English, the State of the Art*. London: Routledge.

Beard, R. (1999) National Literacy Strategy: Review of Research and other Related Evidence. DfEE and Standards and Effectiveness Unit.

Bennett, N. and Kell, J. (1989) *A Good Start? Four Year Olds in Infant Schools*, Oxford: Blackwell.

Bereiter, C. and Scardamalia, M. (1982) From conversation to composition: the role of instruction in a developmental process, in R. Glaser (ed.) *Advances in Instructional Psychology*. Hillsdale, N.J: Lawrence Erlbaum.

Bereiter, C. and Scardamalia, M. (1993) Composing and writing, in R. Beard (ed.) *Teaching Literacy: Balancing Perspectives*. London: Hodder and Stoughton.

Berwick-Emms, P. (1989) Classroom patterns of interaction and their underlying structure: a study of how achievement in the first year of school is influenced by home patterns of interaction. Unpublished Ph.D. thesis. Christchurch: University of Canterbury.

Bielby, N. (1999) *Teaching Reading at Key Stage 2*. Cheltenham: Stanley Thornes.

Bissex, G. (1980) *GNYS AT WRK: A Child Learns to Write and Read*. Cambridge, Mass: Harvard University Press.

Bradley, L. and Bryant, P.E. (1985) *Children's Reading Problems*. Oxford: Basil Blackwell.

Bradley, L. and Bryant, P.E. (1985) *Rhyme and Reason in Reading and Spelling*.

Ann Arbor, MI: University of Michigan Press.

Britton, J. (1972) What's the use? A schematic account of language functions in A. Cashdan and E. Grugeon (eds.) *Language in Education*. London: Routledge.

Britton, J. (1983) Shaping at the point of utterance, in A. Freedman, J. Pringle and J. Yaldin (eds.) *Learning to Write: First Language/Second Language*. London: Longman.

Browne, A. (1992) *Zoo*. London: Red Fox.

Brownjohn, S. (1994) *To Rhyme Or Not To Rhyme*. London: Hodder and Stoughton.

Bruner, J.S. (1957) Going beyond the information given, in H. Gruber (ed.) *Contemporary Approaches to Cognition*. Cambridge, Mass: Harvard University Press.

Burningham, J. (1978) *Would You Rather?* London: Jonathan Cape.

Callagan, M. and Rothery, J. (1988) *Teaching Factual Writing: A Genre Based Approach. Report of the DSP Literacy Project*. Sydney: Metropolitan East Region. NSW Department of Education.

Carter, R. (1990) The new grammar teaching, in R. Carter (ed.) *Knowledge about Language and the Curriculum: The LINC Reader*. Sevenoaks: Hodder and Stoughton.

Carruthers, A. (1991) *The Word Process*, cited in J. Smith, and W. Elley (1998) *How Children Learn to Write*. London: Paul Chapman.

Christie, F. (1994) The Place of Genres in Teaching Critical Social Literacy, in A. Littlefair (ed.) *Literacy for Life*. UK: UKRA.

Clay, M. (1966) *Emergent Reading Behaviour*. Unpublished Doctoral Dissertation. New Zealand: Auckland University.

Clay, M. (1975) *What Did I Write?* London: Heinemann.

Clay, M.M. (1987) Implementing reading recovery: systematic adaptations to an education innovation. *New Zealand Journal of Education Studies* 22(1).

Clay, M.M. (1991) *Becoming Literate: The Construction of Inner Control*. London: Heinemann.

Clay, M.M.(1993) *An Observational Survey of Early Literacy Achievement*. Hong Kong: Heinemann.

Clay, M.M. (1998) *By Different Paths to Common Outcomes*. York, Maine: Stenhouse.

Collerson, J. (ed.) (1988) *Writing and Life*. Sydney: PETA.

Corbett, P. and Moses, B. (1986) *Catapults and Kingfishers*. Oxford: Oxford University Press.

Czerniewska, P. (1992) *Learning about Writing*. Oxford: Blackwell.

DES (1975) *A Language for Life*. (The Bullock Report) London: HMSO.

DES (1984) *English from 5–16*. London: HMSO.

DES (1988) *English 5–16*. London: HMSO.

DES (1989) *English in the National Curriculum*. London: HMSO.

DFE (1995) *English in the National Curriculum*. London: HMSO.

DfEE (1998) *National Literacy Strategy: Framework for Teaching*. London: HMSO.

DfEE (1999) *The Review of the National Curriculum in England: The Consultation*

Materials. QCA.

Dawes, L. (1995) *Drafting*. York: NATE.

Donaldson, M. (1978) *Children's Minds*. Glasgow: Fontana.

Donaldson, M. and Reid, J. (1985) Language skills and reading: a developmental perspective, in M.M. Clarke (ed.) *New Directions in the Study of Reading*. London and Philadelphia: Falmer Press.

Donaldson, M. (1993) Sense and sensibility: some thoughts on the teaching of literacy, in R. Beard (ed.) *Teaching Literacy: Balancing Perspectives*. London: Hodder and Stoughton.

Dyson, A.H. (1989) *Multiple Worlds of Child Writers: Friends Learning to Write*. New York: Teachers College Press.

Education Department of Western Australia (1998) *Writing Developmental Continuum* First Steps Series: Port Melbourne: Rigby Heinemann.

Eggleton, J. M. and Windsor, J. (1995) *Linking the Language Strands*. Auckland: Wings Publication.

Ferreiro, E. (1985) The relationship between oral and written language: the children's viewpoints, in M.M. Clarke (ed.) *New Directions in the Study of Reading*. London and Philadelphia: Falmer Press.

Ferreiro, E. and Teberosky, A. (1982). *Literacy Before Schooling*. London: Heinemann.

Flower, L.S. and Hayes, J.R. (1980a) Writing as problem-solving, *Visible Language* 14(4): 388–99.

Flower, L.S. and Hayes, J.R. (1980b) The dynamics of composing; making plans and juggling constraints, in L.W. Gregg and E.R. Steinberg (eds.) *Cognitive Processes in Writing*. Hillsdale, New Jersey: Lawrence Erlbaum Associates.

Flower, L.S. and Hayes, J.R. (1981) A cognitive process of writing. *College Composition and Communication*. Vol. 32, pp. 365–86.

Foggin, J. (1991) *Real Writing*, Sevenoaks: Hodder and Stoughton.

Frith, U. (1985) Beneath the surface of dyslexia, in K.E. Patterson, M. Coltheart, and J. Marshall, (eds.) 1985 *Surface Dyslexia*, London: LEA.

Gentry, J.R. (1981) Learning to spell developmentally, *Reading Teacher* 34(4), pp. 378–81.

Goodman, K.S. (1973) Psycholinguistic universals in the reading process, in F. Smith (ed.) *Psycholinguistics and Reading*. New York: Holt Rhinehart and Winston.

Goodman, Y. (1984) The Development of Initial Literacy, in F. Smith, H.A. Goelman and A. Oberg (eds.) *Awakening to Literacy*. London: Heinemann.

Goodman, Y. (1991) The development of initial literacy, in R. Carter (ed.) *Knowledge about Language and the Curriculum, The LINC Reader*. Sevenoaks: Hodder and Stoughton.

Graves, D.H. (1983) *Writing: Teachers and Children at Work*. Exeter: Heinemann Education Books.

HMI (1984) *English from 5 to 16*. London: HMSO.

Halliday, M.A.K. (1975) *Learning How to Mean: Explorations in the Development of Language*. London: Edward Arnold.

Halliday, M.A.K. (1978) *Language as a Social Semiotic: The Social Interpretation of Language and Meaning.* London: Edward Arnold.

Halliday, M.A.K. (1985) *An Introduction to Functional Grammar.* London: Edward Arnold.

Halliday, M.A.K. (1989) Context of situation, in M.A.K. Halliday and R. Hasan (eds.) *Language, Context and Text: Aspects of Language in a Social-Semiotic Perspective.* Oxford: Oxford University Press.

Hardy, B. (1977) Towards a poetics of fiction: an approach through narrative, in M. Meek, A. Warlow, G. Barton (eds.) *The Cool Web: The Pattern of Children's Reading.* London: Bodley Head.

Hayes, J.R. and Flower, L.S. (1980) Identifying the organization of writing process, in L. Gregg and E. Steinberg (eds.) *Cognitive Processes in Writing.* New Jersey: Lawrence Erlbaum.

Heath, S.B. (1982) What no bedtime story means: narrative skills at home and school, *Language in Society* 11, pp. 49–76.

Holbrook, D. (1961) *English for Maturity.* Cambridge.

Holdaway, D. (1979) *Foundations of Literacy.* Gosford, NSW: Scholastic Publications.

Hood, H. (1995) *Left to Write.* Auckland: Berkeley Publishing.

Hughes, M. (1986) *Children and Number: Difficulties in Learning Mathematics.* Oxford: Blackwell.

Hull, R. (1988) *Behind The Poem.* London: Routledge.

Hunt, P., Joyner, J. and Stephens, J. (1987) *The English Curriculum: Poetry.* ILEA.

Huxley, A. (1963) *Writers at Work.* 2nd series.

Kinneavy, J.L., Cope, J.Q. and Campbell, J.W. (1976) *Writing – Basic Modes of Organisation.* Duberque, Iowa: Kendall Hunt Publishing Co.

Kress, G. (1982) *Learning to Write.* London: Routledge.

Kress, G. (1987) Genre in a social theory of language, in I. Reid (ed.) *The Place of Genre in Learning.* Sydney: Deakin University.

Kress, G. and Knapp, P. (1992) Genre in a social theory of language, *English Education,* 26(2), pp. 5–15.

Lewis, M. and Wray, D. (1995) *Developing Children's Non-Fiction Writing: Working with Writing Frames.* Leamington Spa: Scholastic.

LINC (1992a) *Broadsheets.* LINC Inner London.

LINC (1992b) *Training Materials.* Unpublished.

Littlefair, A.B. (1992) *Games in the classroom. Minibook 1.* Warrington: UKRA.

Littlefair, A.B. (1993) The 'Good Book': Non-Narrative Aspects in R. Beard (ed.) *Teaching Literacy: Balancing Perspectives.* Sevenoaks, Hodder & Stoughton.

Longacre, R. (1976) *An Anatomy of Speech Notions.* Lisse: Peter de Riddes.

Macken, M. *et al.* (1989) *The Theory and Practice of Genre Based Writing.* Sydney: Literary and Education Research Network, Directorate of Studies, NSW Department of Education.

Mallett, M. (1992) *Making Facts Matter.* London: Paul Chapman.

Martin, J.R. (1984) Types of Writing in Infant Schools, in L. Unsworth, *Reading, Writing, Spelling: Proceedings of the Fifth MacArthur Reading Language*

Symposium. Sydney: MacArthur Institute of Higher Education.

Martin, J.R. and Rothery, J. (1980) *Writing Project Report No. 1*. Sydney: Department of Linguistics, University of Sydney.

Martin, J.R. and Rothery, J. (1981) *Writing Project Report No. 2*. Sydney: Department of Linguistics, University of Sydney.

Martin, J.R. and Rothery, J. (1986) *Writing Project Report No. 4*. Sydney: Department of Linguistics, University of Sydney.

Martin, J.R., Christie, F. and Rothery, J. (1987) Social processes in education, in I. Reid (ed.) *The Place of Genre in Learning*. Sydney: Deakin University.

Martin, J.R., Christie, F. and Rothery, J. (1994) Social Processes in Education: A reply to Sawyer and Watson *et al.*, in B. Stierer and J. Maybin (eds.) (1994) *Language, Literacy and Learning in Educational Practice*. Multilingual Matters Ltd: Open University Press.

McNaughton, S. (1994) Why there might be several ways to read storybooks to preschoolers in Aeoteara/New Zealand: models of tutoring and socio-cultural diversity in how families read books to preschoolers, in Kohl de Olivera and J. Valsinor (eds.) *Literacy Development in Human Development*. Norwood, NJ: Ablex.

McNaughton, S. (1995) *Patterns of Emergent Literacy: Processes of Development and Transition*. Auckland: Oxford University Press.

McNaughton, S., Parr, J. and Smith, L.T. (1966) Processes of Teaching and Learning in Literacy Writing. Final Report to Ministry of Education. Research Project No. ER35/5335. Wellington: Ministry of Education.

Meek, M. (1988) *How Texts Teach What Readers Learn*. Stroud: Thimble Press.

Meek, M. (1996) *Information and Book Learning*. Gloucester: Thimble Press.

NATE (1987) *Exploring Poetry 5–8*. NATE.

Purcell-Gates, V. (1996) Stories, Coupons and the TV Guide: Relationship between home literacy experiences and emergent literacy knowledge, *Reading Research Quarterly*, 31, (4), pp. 406–28.

QCA (1998) *Can do Better: Raising Boys' Achievement in English*. London: QCA.

Richmond, J. (1990) What do we mean by Knowledge about Language? in R. Carter (ed.) *Knowledge about Language and the Curriculum, the LINC Reader*. London: Hodder and Stoughton.

Riley, J.L. (1995a) The transition phase between emergent literacy and conventional beginning reading: new research findings. *TACTYC* (Journal for Tutors for Advanced Courses for Teachers of Young Children) 16 (1), pp. 55–59.

Riley, J.L. (1995b) The relationship between adjustment to school and success in reading by the end of the reception year, *Early Child Development and Care*, 114, pp. 25–38.

Riley, J.L. (1996) *The Teaching of Reading: The Development of Literacy in the Early Years of School*. London: Paul Chapman.

Riley, J.L. (1999) *Teaching Reading at Key Stage 1 and Before*. Cheltenham: Stanley Thornes.

Rosen, M. (1981) *I See a Voice*. London: Thames Hutchinson.

Scardamalia, M. and Bereiter, C. (1986) Research in written composition, in

M. Wittrock (ed.) *Handbook of Research on Teaching, 3rd edn.*, American Educational Research Association. New York: Macmillan.

SCAA (1995b) Planning in Key Stage One and Two. London: SCAA.

Scottish Certificate of Education, Standard Grade (SSG) 1987) *Revised Arrangements for English.* Scottish Examination Board.

Sealey, A. (1996) *Learning about Language: Issues for Primary Teachers.* Oxford: Oxford University Press.

Senechal, M., Lefevre, J., Thomas, E. and Daley, K.E. (1998) Differential effects of home literacy experiences on the development of oral and written language, in *Reading Research Quarterly*, 33, (1), pp. 96–116.

Smith, J. and Elley, W. (1998) *How Children Learn to Write.* London: Paul Chapman.

Sulzby, E. and Teale, W. (1991) Emergent literacy, in J. Barr, M. Kamil, P. Mosenthal and D. Pearson (eds.) *The Handbook of Reading Research.* 2. London: Longman.

Taylor, D. and Dorsey-Gaines, C. (1988) *Growing up Literate.* Portsmouth, NH: Heinemann.

Thompson, D. (ed.) (1969) *Directions in the Teaching of English.* Cambridge.

Tizard, B. and Hughes, M. (1984) *Young Children Learning.* London: Fontana.

Vygotsky, L.S. (1962) *Thought and Language.* Cambridge, Mass: MIT Press.

Vygotsky, L.S. (1978) *Mind in Society: The Development of Higher Psychological Processes.* Cambridge, Mass: Harvard University Press.

Washtell, A. (1998) Routines and resources, in J. Graham and A. Kelly (eds.) *Writing under Control: Teaching Writing in the Primary School.* London: David Fulton.

Wells, C.G. (1985a) *Language, Learning and Education: Selected papers from the Bristol Study 'Language at Home and at School'.* Windsor: NFER-Nelson.

Wells, C.G. (1985b). Pre-school literacy related activities and success in school, in G. Oleon, N. Torrance and A. Hildyard (eds.) *Literacy, Language and Learning: The Nature and Consequences of Reading and Writing.* Cambridge: Cambridge University Press.

Wells, C.G. (1987) *The Meaning Makers: Children Learning Language and Using Language to Learn.* London: Hodder and Stoughton.

Wilkinson, A. (1990) *Argument as Primary Act of Mind, English in Education.* NATE.

Wing Jan, L. (1991) *Write Ways: Modelling Writing Forms.* Melbourne: Oxford University Press.

Wray, D. and Lewis, M. (1997) *Extending Literacy: Children Reading and Writing Non-Fiction.* London: Routledge.

Index